DERIVE

Lab Manual for

CALCULUS

Larson / Hostetler / Edwards

Calculus Series

Houghton Mifflin Company   Boston   New York

Editor in Chief, Mathematics: Charles Hartford
Managing Editor: Cathy Cantin
Senior Associate Editor: Maureen Brooks
Associate Editor: Michael Richards
Assistant Editor: Carolyn Johnson
Supervising Editor: Karen Carter
Art Supervisor: Gary Crespo
Marketing Manager: Sara Whittern
Associate Marketing Manager: Ros Kane
Marketing Assistant: Carrie Lipscomb
Design: Henry Rachlin
Composition and Art: Meridian Creative Group

Trademark Acknowledgments: Derive is a registered trademark of Soft Warehouse, Inc.

Photos courtesy of:
    COREL PROFESSIONAL PHOTOS CD-ROM: Labs P.1, 1.1, 3.1, 5.1, 6.2, 8.2, 10.1, 11.1, 11.2, 12.1, and 15.1
    United States Department of the Interior (Bureau of Reclamation): Lab 6.1
    Meridian Creative Group, a Division of Larson Texts, Inc.: Labs 2.1, 2.2, 4.1, 7.1, 8.1, 13.1, and 14.1
    NASA: Lab 9.1

Printed in the U.S.A.

ISBN: 0-395-88774-7

123456789–B–01 00 99 98 97

Preface

Derive Lab Manual for Calculus accompanies the Larson/Hostetler/Edwards calculus series. It contains 20 labs that, with the aid of technology, can further your understanding of calculus.

Each lab begins with an introduction that includes background information, observations, a statement of the lab's purpose, and one or two references for further investigation on the lab's topic. The lab continues with a presentation of the data described in the introduction, using verbal descriptions, tables, and graphs. The lab concludes with a variety of open-ended exercises that are challenging, analytical, thought-provoking, comparative, and exploratory to give you a deeper understanding of the current topic and of calculus. The accompanying disk contains the files required for each lab. In most cases, the data is stored in the *Derive* file allowing you to focus on problem solving instead of data entry. Also included are commands to aid you in solving some of the exercises (marked with a ⌺). You only need to evaluate the commands or edit the numeric input values and then evaluate the commands. Instructions on how to use the *Derive* files for each lab are stored in a text file. Every effort has been made to make sure that the lab's files work well and run smoothly.

Any comments or suggestions you have for improving this manual are greatly appreciated. *Derive Lab Manual for Calculus* is the result of the efforts of Meridian Creative Group, a Division of Larson Texts, Inc.

Meridian Creative Group,
A Division of Larson Texts, Inc.
5178 Station Road
Erie, PA 16510-4636

Contents

MODELING OLD FAITHFUL'S ERUPTIONS
Modeling Data

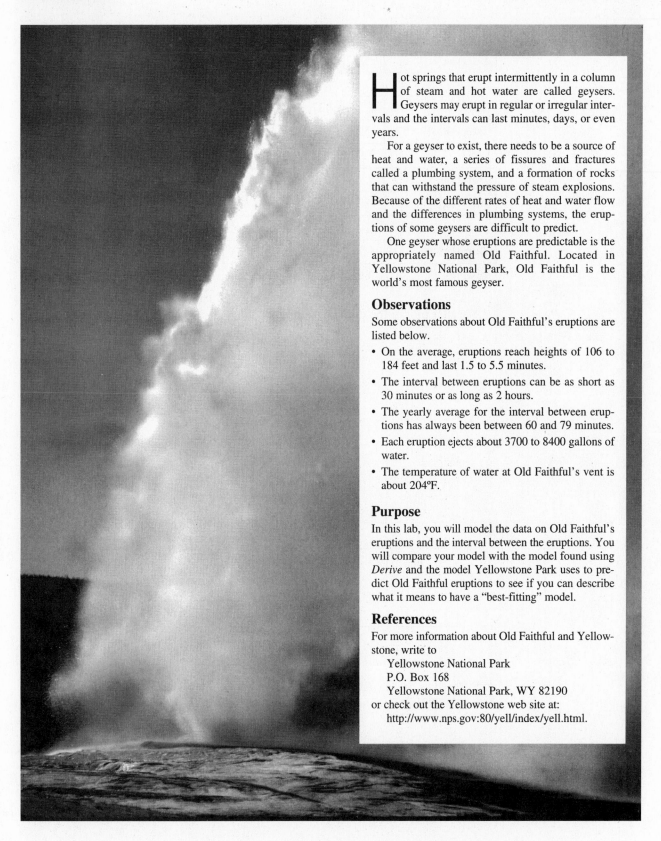

Hot springs that erupt intermittently in a column of steam and hot water are called geysers. Geysers may erupt in regular or irregular intervals and the intervals can last minutes, days, or even years.

For a geyser to exist, there needs to be a source of heat and water, a series of fissures and fractures called a plumbing system, and a formation of rocks that can withstand the pressure of steam explosions. Because of the different rates of heat and water flow and the differences in plumbing systems, the eruptions of some geysers are difficult to predict.

One geyser whose eruptions are predictable is the appropriately named Old Faithful. Located in Yellowstone National Park, Old Faithful is the world's most famous geyser.

Observations

Some observations about Old Faithful's eruptions are listed below.

- On the average, eruptions reach heights of 106 to 184 feet and last 1.5 to 5.5 minutes.
- The interval between eruptions can be as short as 30 minutes or as long as 2 hours.
- The yearly average for the interval between eruptions has always been between 60 and 79 minutes.
- Each eruption ejects about 3700 to 8400 gallons of water.
- The temperature of water at Old Faithful's vent is about 204°F.

Purpose

In this lab, you will model the data on Old Faithful's eruptions and the interval between the eruptions. You will compare your model with the model found using *Derive* and the model Yellowstone Park uses to predict Old Faithful eruptions to see if you can describe what it means to have a "best-fitting" model.

References

For more information about Old Faithful and Yellowstone, write to

Yellowstone National Park
P.O. Box 168
Yellowstone National Park, WY 82190

or check out the Yellowstone web site at:

http://www.nps.gov:80/yell/index/yell.html.

The duration of Old Faithful's eruptions and the interval between the eruptions is given in the table below. Let x represent the duration of a geyser eruption in minutes. Let y represent the interval between geyser eruptions in minutes.

Duration, x	1.80	1.82	1.88	1.90	1.92	1.93	1.98	2.03	2.05	2.13
Interval, y	56	58	60	62	60	56	57	60	57	60

Duration, x	2.30	2.35	2.37	2.82	3.13	3.27	3.65	3.70	3.78	3.83
Interval, y	57	57	61	73	76	77	77	82	79	85

Duration, x	3.87	3.88	4.10	4.27	4.30	4.30	4.43	4.43	4.47	4.47
Interval, y	81	80	89	90	84	89	84	89	86	80

Duration, x	4.53	4.55	4.60	4.60	4.63
Interval, y	89	86	88	92	91

A scatter plot of the data is given below.

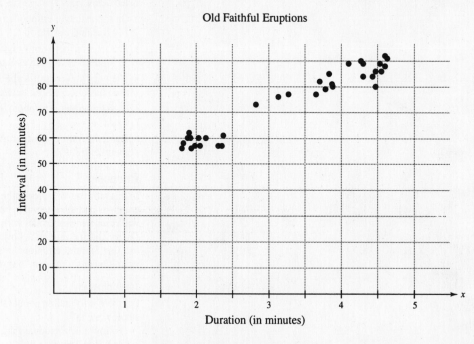

The data in the table and the scatter plot are stored in the *Derive* file called LAB0P01.MTH. The instructions for this *Derive* file are stored in the text file called LAB0P01.TXT.

Name _____

Date _____ Class _____

Instructor _____

1. *Describe the Relationship.*   Describe in words the numerical relationship between x and y as given in this lab's Data. Also suggest a possible explanation of why x and y are related in this manner.

_____

_____

_____

_____

_____

_____

_____

_____

_____

_____

_____

_____

_____

_____

_____

_____

_____

_____

_____

_____

_____

2. Drawing a Best-Fitting Line.   Draw the line that seems to best fit the data points and find its equation (by hand).

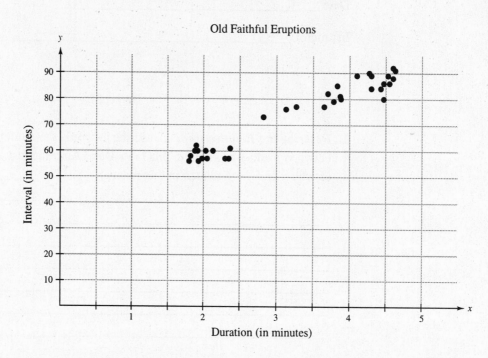

Old Faithful Eruptions

3. Is Your Model the Best?   Use the table given in this lab's Data and *Derive* to compare the actual *y*-values and your equation's *y*-values. How good is your model? Do you think it is the best possible linear model? Explain your reasoning.

_____

_____

_____

_____

_____

_____

4. Smaller or Larger Sum?   In this lab's *Derive* file the sum of the squares of the differences of the actual *y*-values and your equation's *y*-values is given. If you could find a better fitting linear model, would its sum be smaller or larger than the sum that is given? Explain your reasoning.

_____

_____

_____

_____

_____

_____

5. **"Least Squares" Method.** In statistics the linear model that best fits the data is found using what is called a "least squares" method. Based on your answer to Exercise 4, what do you think this means?

_____

_____

_____

_____

_____

_____

_____

6. **_Comparing Equations._** The equation used by Yellowstone Park to predict the intervals between Old Faithful's eruptions is $y = 14x + 30$. Compare this equation with the one you found in Exercise 2. Which equation seems to be the "better" model? Explain your reasoning.

_____

_____

_____

_____

_____

_____

_____

7. **_Choosing the Best Model._** In this lab's _Derive_ file, the least squares method is used to find the "best" linear model for the Old Faithful eruption data. Use the table to compare the actual y-values and the least squares model's y-values. Of these two linear models and your own, which is the best one? Why?

_____

_____

_____

_____

_____

_____

_____

8. *Lab Summary.* Summarize your results and sketch the graph of each.

Model from Exercise 2: _____

Yellowstone Park Model: _____

Least Squares Model: _____

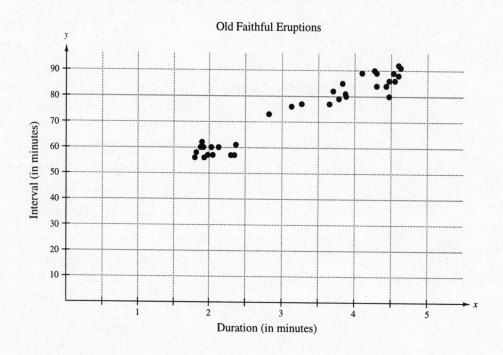

Old Faithful Eruptions

9. *A Better Type of Model?* Do you think a quadratic model would fit the data better than a linear model in this case? Why or why not?

_____

_____

_____

_____

_____

_____

_____

_____

It is often said in sports that records are made to be broken. This saying suggests there is no limit to athletic performance.

In some sports, such as the men's 100-meter freestyle, the record time is no longer being broken as often or by as much as in the past.

Observations

The men's 100-meter freestyle record in 1956 was 55.4 seconds. By 1976 the record had dropped about 10.8% to 49.44 seconds. In that period, new records had been set 17 times.

Since then, there has not been as much improvement on the record. The record time has only dropped about 2.5% since 1976 to 48.21 seconds and new records have been set six times.

Purpose

In this lab, you will analyze the record times of the men's 100-meter freestyle to determine if there is a lower limit on the time it takes a man to swim 100 meters. You will be given an equation that models the record times and find its lower limit graphically, numerically, and analytically. You will use *Derive* to verify your results.

References

For more information about swimming and its records, visit Swimnews online at :

http://www.swimnews.com.

The year of a record set in the men's 100-meter freestyle and the record time in seconds is given in the table below. Let x represent the year, where $x = 0$ corresponds to 1900. Let y represent the record time in seconds.

Year, x	56	57	57	61	61	64	67	68	70
Time, y	55.4	55.2	54.6	54.4	53.6	52.9	52.6	52.2	51.9

Year, x	72	72	75	75	75	76	76	76	81
Time, y	51.47	51.22	51.12	51.11	50.59	50.39	49.99	49.44	49.36

Year, x	85	85	86	88	94
Time, y	49.24	48.95	48.74	48.42	48.21

A scatter plot of the data is given below.

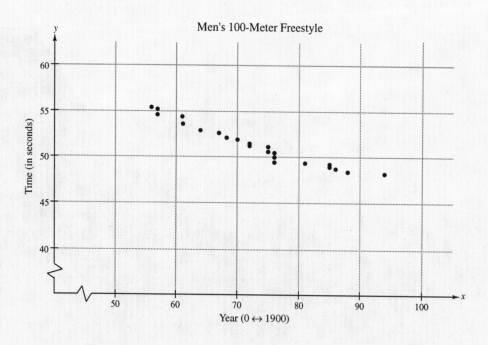

The data in the table and the scatter plot are stored in the *Derive* file called LAB0101.MTH. The instructions for this *Derive* file are stored in the text file called LAB0101.TXT.

Name _____

Date _____ Class _____

Instructor _____

1. *Limited or Unlimited?*   Is there a limit to human athletic performance or is there no limit? List several reasons why you think there is a limit or several reasons why you think there isn't a limit to human athletic performance.

_____
_____
_____
_____
_____
_____
_____
_____
_____
_____
_____

2. *Graphical Estimation.*   Use the scatter plot given in this lab's Data to estimate a reasonable lower limit on the time it takes a man to swim 100 meters. Explain how you determined this limit. Predict the record for the men's 100-meter freestyle in the year 2000.

_____
_____
_____
_____
_____
_____
_____
_____
_____
_____
_____

3. *Analytical Estimation.* A model for the men's 100-meter freestyle record times in seconds is given by

$$y = \frac{38{,}504.4888 + 44.37530536x^2}{1 + x + x^2},$$

where $x = 0$ represents 1900. The model and the data points are shown in the graph below. Use this model to predict a reasonable record for a man to swim 100 meters in the year 2000. Explain how you determined your answer.

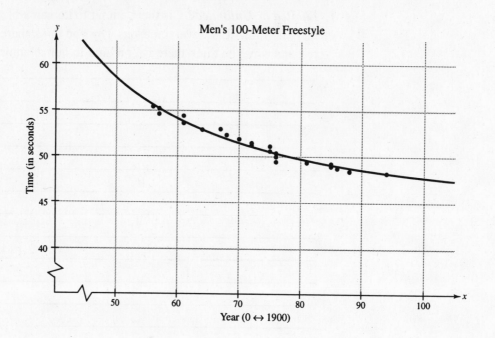

_____

_____

_____

_____

_____

_____

_____

_____

_____

_____

_____

_____

_____

_____

_____

4. Numerical Estimation. In this lab's *Derive* file, the limit of the model

$$y = \frac{38,504.4888 + 44.37530536x^2}{1 + x + x^2}$$

is given as x approaches 100. Compare this estimation of the record for the men's 100-meter freestyle record time in 2000 with those you found in Exercises 2 and 3. Which estimate seems more reasonable to you? Why?

_____

_____

_____

_____

_____

_____

_____

_____

_____

_____

_____

5. Complete the Table. In this lab's *Derive* file, the limit of the model

$$y = \frac{38,504.4888 + 44.37530536x^2}{1 + x + x^2}$$

is given as x approaches 100. Write the result of this calculation in the table below. Edit the *Derive* file to find the limit of the model for the remaining values of x given in the table. Record the results below.

Year, x	100	150	200	250	300
Time, y					

What conclusions can you make about the existence of a lower limit on the time it takes a man to swim 100 meters?

_____

_____

_____

_____

_____

_____

_____

_____

_____

6. A Model for all Years? Do you think the model

$$y = \frac{38{,}504.4888 + 44.37530536x^2}{1 + x + x^2}$$

is a good estimation of record times for any year or is the model only good for particular years? Explain how you reached your conclusion and determine which years the model could be used to estimate record times. Use *Derive* to analyze the model graphically and numerically. (Note: In 1905 the men's 100-meter freestyle record was 1:05.8 or 65.8 seconds.)

_____

_____

_____

_____

_____

_____

_____

_____

_____

_____

_____

_____

_____

7. Enough Proof? Do you think the results of this lab are enough to prove that there is a limit to how fast a man can swim 100 meters? Why or why not?

_____

_____

_____

_____

_____

_____

_____

_____

_____

_____

_____

_____

FALLING OBJECTS

First and Second Derivatives

To study the motion of an object under the influence of gravity, we need equipment to track the motion of the object. We can use calculus to analyze the data. Calculus can be used to determine the object's position, velocity, and acceleration due to gravity.

Observations

In theory, the position of a free-falling object (neglecting air resistance) is given by

$$s(t) = \frac{1}{2}gt^2 + v_0 t + s_0,$$

where g is the acceleration due to gravity, t is the time, v_0 is the initial velocity, and s_0 is the initial height.

Purpose

In this lab, you will analyze the data of a free-falling object collected during an experiment. You will use the first and second derivative and *Derive* to study the motion of the object.

References

For more information about experiments involving the study of motion of an object, see *CBL Explorations in Calculus* by Meridian Creative Group.

Data

The positions of a falling ball at time intervals of 0.02 second are given in the table below.

Time (sec)	Height (meters)	Velocity (meters/sec)
0.00	0.290864	−0.16405
0.02	0.284279	−0.32857
0.04	0.274400	−0.49403
0.06	0.260131	−0.71322
0.08	0.241472	−0.93309
0.10	0.219520	−1.09409
0.12	0.189885	−1.47655
0.14	0.160250	−1.47891
0.16	0.126224	−1.69994
0.18	0.086711	−1.96997
0.20	0.045002	−2.07747
0.22	0.000000	−2.25010

Scatter plots of the data are given below.

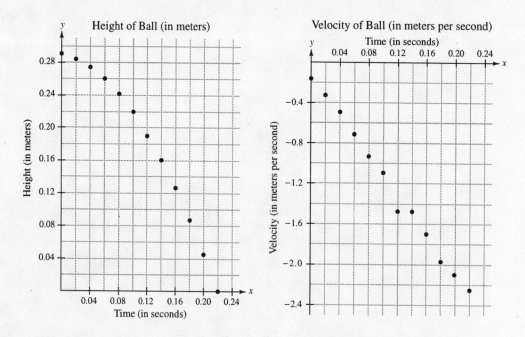

The data in the table and the scatter plot are stored in the *Derive* file called LAB0201.MTH. The instructions for this *Derive* file are stored in the text file called LAB0201.TXT.

Exercises

Name _____

Date _____ Class _____

Instructor _____

1. *What Type of Model?*   What type of model seems to be the best fit for the scatter plot of the heights of the falling ball? What type of model seems to be the best fit for the scatter plot of the velocity of the falling ball? Describe any relationships you see between the two models.

_____

_____

_____

_____

_____

_____

_____

_____

_____

_____

_____

_____

2. *Modeling the Position Function.*   A model of a position function takes the form

$$s(t) = \frac{1}{2}gt^2 + v_0 t + s_0.$$

Use *Derive* to find the position function of the falling ball described in this lab's Data and record the result below. Use this position function to determine the ball's initial height, initial velocity, velocity function, and acceleration function and record the results below.

Position Function: $s(t) =$

Initial Height: $s_0 =$

Initial Velocity: $v_0 =$

Velocity Function: $v(t) = s'(t) =$

Acceleration Function: $a(t) = s''(t) =$

3. *A Good Fit?* Is the velocity function you found in Exercise 2 a good fit? Why or why not? Use *Derive* to analyze the velocity function graphically and numerically.

_____

_____

_____

_____

_____

_____

_____

_____

_____

_____

4. *Modeling the Velocity Function.* A model of a velocity function takes the form

$$v(t) = gt + v_0.$$

Use *Derive* to find the velocity function of the falling ball described in this lab's Data and record the result below. Use this velocity function to determine the acceleration function and record the result below.

Velocity Function: $v(t) =$

Acceleration Function: $a(t) = v'(t) =$

5. *What's the Difference?* Of the velocity functions you found in Exercises 2 and 4, which one is a better fit to the data? Use *Derive* to analyze the velocity functions graphically and numerically. Explain why these velocity functions which describe the same data are different.

_____

_____

_____

_____

_____

_____

_____

_____

_____

6. *Estimating Earth's Gravity.* Of the acceleration functions you found in Exercises 2 and 4, which one is closer to the actual value of earth's gravity? (Note: The value of earth's gravity is approximately -9.8 m/sec^2.) Calculate the percent error of the closest estimate of earth's gravity. Do you think this is a good estimate? Why or why not?

_____

_____

_____

_____

_____

_____

_____

_____

_____

_____

_____

_____

_____

Another Ball. For Exercises 7–9, use the following data.

Time (sec)	Height (meters)	Time (sec)	Height (meters)
0.00	0.806736	0.32	1.149180
0.02	0.857225	0.34	1.141500
0.04	0.904422	0.36	1.126130
0.06	0.946131	0.38	1.105280
0.08	0.985644	0.40	1.082230
0.10	1.020760	0.42	1.056980
0.12	1.052590	0.44	1.026250
0.14	1.080030	0.46	0.992230
0.16	1.103080	0.48	0.954912
0.18	1.122840	0.50	0.913203
0.20	1.137110	0.52	0.868201
0.22	1.149180	0.54	0.819907
0.24	1.156870	0.56	0.767222
0.26	1.160160	0.58	0.711244
0.28	1.161260	0.60	0.651974
0.30	1.156870	0.62	0.589411

7. Use *Derive* to find a model for the position function of the data and record the result below. Use this position function to determine the ball's initial height and initial velocity. Do you think this ball was dropped or thrown? Explain your reasoning.

Position Function: $s(t) =$

Initial Height: $s_0 =$

Initial Velocity: $v_0 =$

_____

_____

_____

_____

_____

_____

_____

8. Use *Derive* to analyze the graph of the position function s from Exercise 7 and its derivative s'. For which values of the time t is s' positive? For which values of the time t is s' negative? What does the graph of s' tell you about the graph of s?

_____

_____

_____

_____

_____

_____

_____

9. Use *Derive* to analyze the tangent line to the graph of the position function s from Exercise 7 at different times. At what time is the slope of the tangent line horizontal? What is the velocity of the ball at this time?

_____

_____

_____

_____

_____

_____

_____

Robert Boyle (1627–1691), who is often considered the founder of modern chemistry, made studies of acids and bases, the calcination of metals, combustion, the nature of colors, and the propagation of sound. Boyle is best known for his experiments on gases and the formulation of the gas law that bears his name.

Observations

A unique property of a gas is that it is compressible. A given volume of a gas, unlike a solid or a liquid, can be squeezed into a smaller container or compressed by the application of pressure. As the volume of the gas decreases, the pressure that the gas exerts on its container increases. Boyle determined, after many experiments, that the volume of a sample of gas at a given temperature varies inversely with the applied pressure.

Purpose

In this lab, you will explore the relationship between the pressure of a trapped gas and its container. You will use *Derive* to aid you in your exploration.

References

For more information about Robert Boyle, *The Life of the Honourable Robert Boyle* by R. E. W. Maddison.

Data

Boyle's Law states that the volume of a sample of gas at a given temperature varies inversely with the applied pressure. Mathematically, Boyle's Law can be written as

$$PV = k \text{ or } V = \frac{k}{P}$$

where V is the volume of the gas, P is the applied pressure, and k is a constant. Boyle's Law is only valid for systems which are at a constant temperature and contain a constant mass of gas. When these conditions are met, the product of the pressure and the volume remains nearly constant. The pressure-volume data in the table below is for 1.000 g of oxygen at 0°C.

Pressure, P (atm)	Volume, V (L)
0.25	2.801
0.50	1.400
0.75	0.9333
1.00	0.6998
2.00	0.3495
3.00	0.2328
4.00	0.1744
5.00	0.1394

A scatter plot of the data is given below.

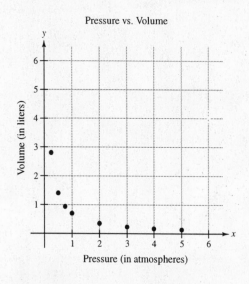

Pressure vs. Volume

The data in the table and the scatter plot is stored in the *Derive* file called LAB0202.MTH. The instructions for this *Derive* file are stored in the text file called LAB0202.TXT.

Name _____

Date _____ Class _____

Instructor _____

1. *Complete the Table.*   Calculate the product of the pressure and the volume (*PV*) for the pressure-volume data discussed in this lab's Data and complete the table below.

Pressure, *P* (atm)	Volume, *V* (L)	*PV*
0.25	2.801	
0.50	1.400	
0.75	0.9333	
1.00	0.6998	
2.00	0.3495	
3.00	0.2328	
4.00	0.1744	
5.00	0.1394	

Is the product of the pressure and the volume approximately equal to a constant number *k*? If so, determine the value of the constant *k* and use *Derive* to graph the equation

$$V = \frac{k}{P}$$

with the pressure-volume data. Use the graph to verbally describe the relationship between the pressure of a collected gas (in this case, oxygen) and its volume. Is the pressure ever zero?

_____

_____

_____

_____

_____

_____

_____

2. Pressure-Volume Relationship. Use *Derive* to graph the pressure-volume data given in this lab's Data with the volume on the vertical axis and $1/P$ on the horizontal axis. Is the data nearly linear? If so, determine the slope of a line that approximates the data. Verbally describe what the slope means in the context of the data. What is the y-intercept of the line? What does the y-intercept mean in the context of the data?

_____

_____

_____

_____

3. Using the Derivative. The equation for Boyle's Law is

$$PV = k.$$

Solve the equation for V and use the derivative to show that the rate of change of the volume with respect to pressure is inversely proportional to the square of the pressure.

4. Graphing the Derivative. Use the result of Exercise 3 to find the derivative dV/dP of

$$V = \frac{k}{P}$$

where k is the value you determined in Exercise 1. Then use *Derive* to graph

$$V = \frac{k}{P}$$

and its derivative on the same coordinate axes. Is the graph of the derivative always negative? Why or why not? What is the relationship between the slope of the derivative's tangent line and the graph of

$$V = \frac{k}{P}?$$

_____

_____

_____

_____

5. *Graphical Estimation.* Use the graph in this lab's Data to estimate the missing volume data in the following table.

Pressure, P (atm)	Volume, V (L)
1.00	0.6998
1.50	
2.00	0.3495
2.50	
3.00	0.2328
3.50	
4.00	0.1744
4.50	

6. *Proof.* Boyle's Law can be used to calculate the volume occupied by a gas when the applied pressure changes. Let P_1 and V_1 be the initial pressure and volume, respectively, of a gas. After a change in pressure from P_1 to P_2, show that the new volume V_2 can be found by the following equation.

$$V_2 = \frac{P_1 V_1}{P_2}$$

7. *Missing Data.* Use the equation given in Exercise 6 to find the missing volume data in the following table.

Pressure, P (atm)	Volume, V (L)
1.00	0.6998
1.50	
2.00	0.3495
2.50	
3.00	0.2328
3.50	
4.00	0.1744
4.50	

8. *Charles's Law.*   In this lab's Data, we stated that Boyle's Law is only valid for systems which are at a constant temperature. Jacques Charles (1746–1823) discovered that the volume of a sample of gas at a constant pressure increases linearly with temperature and can be written as

$$V = mT$$

where V is the volume of the gas, T is the temperature in Kelvins, and m is a constant. After a change in temperature from T_1 to T_2, show that the new volume V_2 can be found by the following equation.

$$V_2 = \frac{T_2 V_1}{T_1}$$

9. *Combining Boyle's Law and Charles's Law.*   Boyle's Law and Charles's Law can be combined and expressed in a single statement: The volume occupied by a sample of gas is proportional to the temperature (in Kelvins) divided by the pressure and can be written as

$$V = k\frac{T}{P}$$

where V is the volume of the gas, T is the temperature in Kelvins, P is the applied pressure, and k is a constant. After a change in temperature from T_1 to T_2 and a change in pressure from P_1 to P_2, show that the new volume V_2 can be found by the following equation.

$$V_2 = \frac{P_1 T_2 V_1}{P_2 T_1}$$

T here are many decisions to be made when designing a package for a product. For example, what will be the shape of the package? How much will the package need to hold? What will be the dimensions of the package? With these questions, it is easy to see that the packaging of some products can be more complicated than the product itself.

Observations

Making packages is a big industry. There are about 500 billion packages used every year in the United States. More than half of these packages contain foods or beverages. Of the 500 billion packages used every year, over 100 billion are cans. It takes 10 million tons of steel to make these cans.

Purpose

In this lab, you will analyze different package shapes and their optimal sizes. You will use the first and second derivative and *Derive* to study the different package shapes.

References

For more information about packaging, see the *Handbook of Package Engineering* from Technomic Publishing.

The table below gives the approximate measurements in inches of several common items packed in cylindrical containers.

Product	Radius (in.)	Height (in.)	Volume (in.³)
Baking powder	1.25	3.65	17.92
Cleanser	1.45	7.50	49.54
Coffee	1.95	5.20	62.12
Coffee creamer	1.50	6.85	48.42
Frosting	1.63	3.60	30.05
Pineapple juice	2.10	6.70	92.82
Soup	1.30	3.80	20.18
Tomato puree	1.95	4.40	52.56

An infinite number of dimensions can be used to construct a right circular container of a given volume. The graph below shows the relationship between the radius and surface area for containers that have a volume of 48.42 cubic inches.

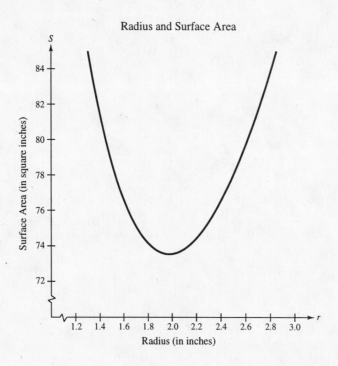

Radius and Surface Area

The data in the table and the scatter plot are stored in the *Derive* file called LAB0301.MTH. The instructions for this *Derive* file are stored in the text file called LAB0301.TXT.

Name _____

Date _____ Class _____

Instructor _____

1. **Complete the Table.** Use the equation for the surface area of a right circular cylinder and the dimensions given in this lab's Data to complete the table.

Surface Area of a Right Circular Cylinder: $S = 2\pi r^2 + 2\pi rh$

Product	Surface Area (in.^{2})
Baking powder	
Cleanser	
Coffee	
Coffee creamer	
Frosting	
Pineapple juice	
Soup	
Tomato puree	

2. **The Only One?** The baking powder container described in this lab's Data has a radius of 1.25 inches, a surface area of 38.48 square inches, and a volume of 17.92 cubic inches. Is it possible to design another baking powder container with the same surface area and volume but a different radius? Why or why not? If it is possible, find the dimensions of another container having a surface area of 38.48 square inches and a volume of 17.92 cubic inches

_____

_____

_____

_____

_____

_____

3. Think About It.   Do you think each of the products listed in Exercise 1 uses a container that minimizes surface area for the volume given in this lab's Data? Why or why not?

_____

_____

_____

_____

_____

_____

4. Designing a Container With a Specified Volume.   Suppose you are designing a baking powder container that has a volume of 17.92 cubic inches. Use the equations for the surface area of a cylinder and the volume of a cylinder to develop an equation relating the surface area S and the radius r. (Note: the volume of a right circular cylinder is $V = \pi r^2 h$.)

Use *Derive* to plot the equation. Determine the radius of the baking powder container that minimizes surface area. Is this radius larger than, smaller than, or equal to the radius given for the baking powder container in this lab's Data? Does the baking powder container given in this lab's Data minimize surface area?

_____

_____

_____

_____

_____

5. Finding the "Optimal" Surface Area.   Repeat Exercise 4 for each of the products listed below and record the "optimal" radius in the table. Then use the volume and radius to determine the height and surface area for each container.

Product	Volume (in.³)	Radius (in.)	Height (in.)	Surface Area (in.²)
Cleanser	49.54			
Coffee	62.12			
Coffee creamer	48.42			
Frosting	30.05			
Pineapple juice	92.82			
Soup	20.18			
Tomato puree	52.56			

6. *A Different Container Shape.* Design a rectangular container with a square base for each of the following volumes and heights. The volume of a rectangular container with a square base is

$$V = x^2h$$

and the surface area is

$$S = x^2 + 4xh.$$

Volume (in.³)	Height (in.)	Side of Base (in.)	Surface Area (in.²)
17.92	3.65		
49.54	7.50		
62.12	5.20		
48.42	6.85		
30.05	3.60		
92.82	6.70		
20.18	3.80		
52.56	4.40		

Compare the rectangular containers with square bases to the cylinders that have the same volume in Exercise 1. What advantages do the rectangular containers have over the cylinders? What disadvantages do they have?

_____

_____

_____

_____

_____

_____

_____

_____

_____

_____

_____

_____

7. **Optimizing a Rectangular Container.** In Exercise 6, did you design each rectangular container such that surface area was minimized? For a fixed volume V, how would you determine the minimum surface area of a rectangular container with a square base? For a fixed surface area S, how would you determine the maximum volume of a rectangular container with a square base?

_____

_____

_____

_____

_____

_____

_____

_____

_____

_____

8. **Why not?** Determine whether the surface area you found in Exercise 1 for each container is equal to the "optimal" surface area you found for each container in Exercise 5. Give several reasons why a company would make a container that does not use an "optimal" surface area.

_____

_____

_____

_____

_____

_____

_____

_____

_____

_____

_____

WANKEL ROTARY ENGINE
Area

While designs for rotary engines date back as far as the 1500's, the Wankel rotary engine was developed by Felix Wankel in the 1950's. The design of the rotary engine uses some interesting geometric shapes. The rotor in a Wankel engine is shaped like a slightly bulged equilateral triangle and the shape of the rotor's housing chamber is an epitrochoid.

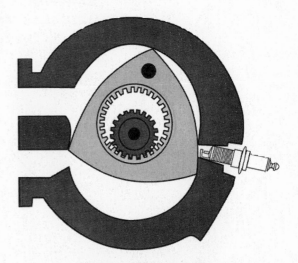

Observations

The Wankel engine has some advantages over the common piston engine. The Wankel engine has fewer moving parts. For example, there are no valves, connecting rods, or timing belts. Thus, the Wankel engine should have less labor and material costs. However, the Wankel engine is less thermodynamically efficient and uses more fuel than most piston engines.

Purpose

In this lab, you will analyze the housing chamber. You will use numerical methods and use *Derive* to study the measurements of a chamber design.

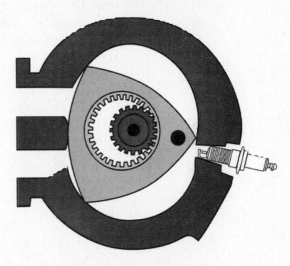

References

For more information about the Wankel rotary engine, see *The Wankel Engine: Design, Development, Application* by Jan D. Norbye.

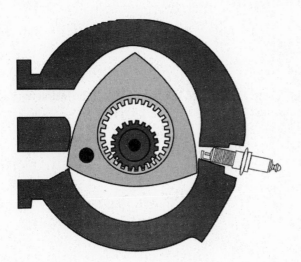

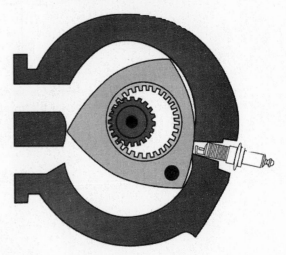

The rotor in a Wankel engine is shaped like a slightly bulged equilateral triangle, as shown in the graph below.

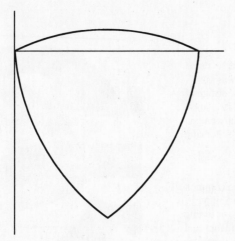

The rotor's housing chamber has the shape of an epitrochoid. An epitrochoid is a curve traced by a point on a circle rolling around another circle without slipping. An example of an epitrochoid is shown below.

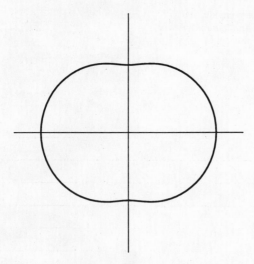

The *Derive* file corresponding to this lab is called LAB0401.MTH. The instructions for this *Derive* file are stored in the text file called LAB0401.TXT.

Name _____

Date _____ Class _____

Instructor _____

1. **Estimating Area.** Use the scale drawing of the rotor to estimate the rotor's area. Explain how you obtained your estimate and approximate the error.

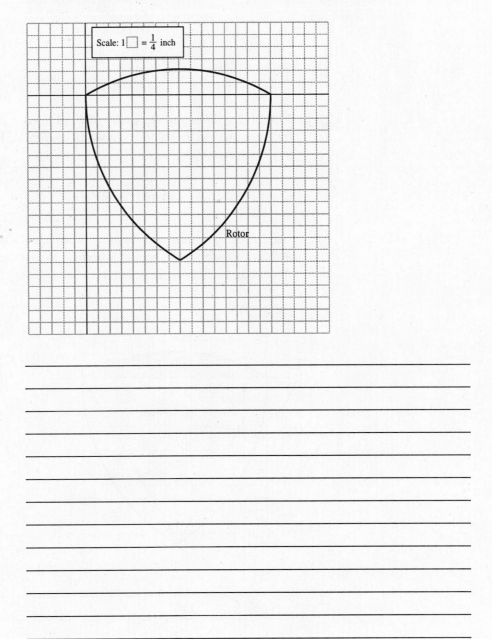

_____

_____

_____

_____

_____

_____

_____

_____

_____

_____

_____

_____

_____

2. *A Reasonable Estimate?* Inscribe and circumscribe an equilateral triangle on the rotor in the figure in Exercise 1. Then find the areas of the triangles. Use these areas to determine if your estimate in Exercise 1 is reasonable.

3. *Using Integration and Geometry to Find Area.* An equilateral triangle has been inscribed in the rotor as shown in the figure. The area of the shaded region is given by

$$\int_0^4 \left(-2\sqrt{3} + \sqrt{16 - (x-2)^2}\right) dx.$$

Use *Derive* to evaluate this integral. Then use the result of the integration and the formula for the area of a triangle to find the total area of the rotor. According to Exercise 2, is this result reasonable?

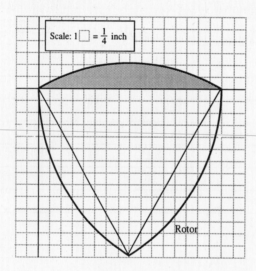

Scale: 1 ☐ = $\frac{1}{4}$ inch

Rotor

4. Using a Numerical Method. Several measurements of a region of a rotor are given in the table. Use the measurements, the Trapezoidal Rule and *Derive* to estimate the area of the region where *x* and *y* are measured in inches as shown in the figure. Determine the possible error of this estimate. Do you think this is an acceptable amount of error? Why or why not? How can the error in the estimate of the region's area be reduced?

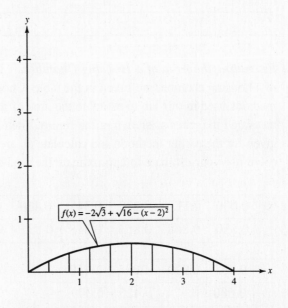

$$f(x) = -2\sqrt{3} + \sqrt{16 - (x-2)^2}$$

x	0.00	0.40	0.80	1.20	1.60	2.00	2.40
y	0.00	0.20	0.35	0.45	0.52	0.54	0.52

x	2.80	3.20	3.60	4.00
y	0.45	0.35	0.20	0.00

5. *Another Numerical Method.* Repeat Exercise 4 using Simpson's Rule and *Derive*. Which method gives a better estimate? If the number of measurements is increased, which method do you think will be better: the Trapezoidal Rule or Simpson's Rule? Explain your reasoning.

_____

_____

_____

_____

6. *Estimating the Area of a Housing Chamber.* The measurements of a region of a housing chamber are given in the table. Choose one of the numerical methods used in this lab to estimate the area of the chamber where x and y are measured in inches as shown in the figure. Then modify the *Derive* commands given for the earlier methods and calculate an area estimate. Explain how you could use your estimate to approximate the area of the entire housing chamber.

x	0.000	0.115	0.230	0.345	0.460	0.575	0.690
y	0.850	0.848	0.854	0.848	0.835	0.804	0.748

x	0.805	0.920	1.035	1.150
y	0.680	0.574	0.425	0.000

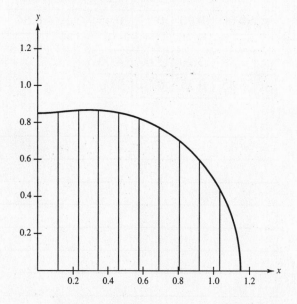

_____

_____

_____

_____

NEWTON'S LAW OF COOLING

Exponential Decay

One common method of shaping plastic products is to pour hot plastic resin into a mold. The resin, which was poured at a temperature of 300°F, is then cooled in a chiller system that is kept at 58°F. After cooling to an appropriate temperature, the molded product is ejected. This is done as quickly as possible to minimize cost and speed up production. Ejecting the product too quickly, however, can introduce warping or punctures.

Observations

The cooling process of plastic resin is an example of a process that obeys Newton's Law of Cooling. This law states that the rate of change in the temperature of an object is proportional to the difference between the object's temperature and the temperature of the surrounding medium. This relationship can be used to model the temperature of the cooling plastic with respect to time.

Purpose

In this lab, you will analyze the temperatures of an experiment and verify that Newton's Law of Cooling applies to the data. You will use *Derive* to verify your results.

References

For more information about collecting data for an experiment on Newton's Law of Cooling, see *CBL Explorations on Calculus* by Meridian Creative Group.

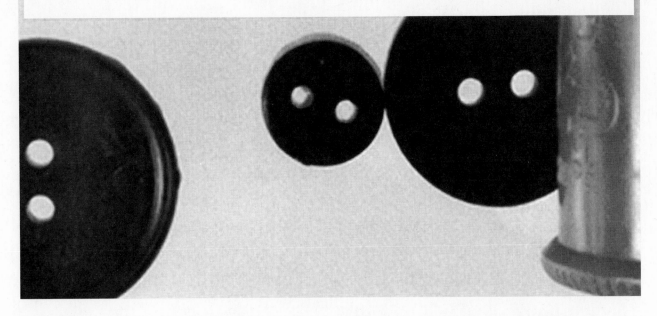

The temperature of a cup of water was taken at two-second intervals during a 44-second period and recorded in the table below. The room temperature was measured at 69.548°F, and the water temperature at time $t = 0$ was measured at 169.628°F. The time t is given in seconds and the temperature T is given in degrees Fahrenheit.

Time, t	0	2	4	6	8	10
Temperature, T	169.628	163.328	156.596	148.280	140.468	133.358

Time, t	12	14	16	18	20	22
Temperature, T	127.634	122.756	118.364	114.620	111.488	108.410

Time, t	24	26	28	30	32	34
Temperature, T	105.638	103.154	100.904	98.924	96.746	94.784

Time, t	36	38	40	42	44
Temperature, T	92.858	91.364	89.672	88.394	87.134

Time and Temperature

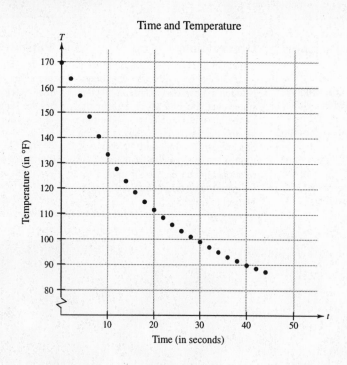

The data in the table and the scatter plot are stored in the *Derive* file called LAB0501.MTH. The instructions for this *Derive* file are stored in the text file called LAB0501.TXT.

Exercises

Name _____

Date _____ Class _____

Instructor _____

1. *Describing What Happened.* Use the scatter plot to describe the rate at which the water cooled. Do you think the temperature of the water ever reached 69.548°F? Why or why not?

_____

_____

_____

_____

_____

_____

_____

_____

_____

2. *Finding a General Solution.* Newton's Law of Cooling can be represented mathematically by the differential equation

$$\frac{dy}{dt} = k(y - L)$$

where y is the temperature of the object at time t, k is a proportionality constant, and L is the temperature of the surrounding medium. Find the general solution of this differential equation. Describe in real-life terms what each unknown represents. Describe what you think the general equation's arbitrary constant represents.

_____

_____

_____

_____

_____

_____

3. *Finding a Particular Solution.* Apply the differential equation and its general solution from Exercise 2 to the temperatures of the water as described in this lab's Data. Show your work and record your results below. Describe in words what the general equation's arbitrary constant represents in the context of this experiment. Does this description confirm or contradict your description in Exercise 2? If it is a contradiction, rewrite the description.

Differential equation: $\dfrac{dy}{dt} =$

General solution: $y =$

Particular solution: $y =$

_____

_____

_____

_____

_____

_____

_____

_____

_____

_____

_____

4. *Will the Water Reach Room Temperature?* Does the temperature of the water ever reach room temperature? Why or why not? Explain how you determined your conclusion. If the water does reach room temperature, find the time t when this occurs. Does this result support the conclusion you drew in Exercise 1?

_____

_____

_____

_____

_____

_____

_____

_____

_____

_____

5. *First Derivative.*   Verbally describe the graph of the first derivative of the particular solution from Exercise 3. Graph the first derivative to verify your description. Explain what the value of the first derivative means at a time *t*.

_____

_____

_____

_____

_____

_____

_____

6. *Second Derivative.*   Verbally describe the graph of the second derivative of the particular solution from Exercise 3. Graph the second derivative to verify your description. Explain what the value of the second derivative means at a time *t*.

_____

_____

_____

_____

_____

_____

_____

7. *Comparing Solutions.*   Use *Derive* to find the general and particular solutions of the differential equation

$$\frac{dy}{dt} = k(y - L)$$

with respect to the temperatures of the water that is described in this lab's Data. Compare the equations *Derive* found to those that you found in Exercise 3. If the equations are different, explain why.

_____

_____

_____

_____

_____

_____

_____

8. **Cooling Plastic.** Apply the differential equation and its general solution from Exercise 2 to the cooling plastic discussed in the Introduction of this lab. Is there enough information to determine the value of the proportionality constant k? If so, find its value. If not, explain what additional information is needed to determine the value of k.

Differential equation: $\dfrac{dy}{dt} =$

General solution: $y =$

Particular solution: $y =$

_____

_____

_____

_____

_____

_____

_____

_____

_____

_____

9. **Is Cooler Better?** If speed of production is important, how could you make the cooling process go faster? Do you think this is a viable solution? Why or why not?

_____

_____

_____

_____

_____

_____

_____

_____

_____

_____

_____

_____

CONSTRUCTING AN ARCH DAM

Surface Area, Volume, and Fluid Force

When designing structures like dams, many questions arise. How much material will be needed to build the structure? If the material used to build the structure needs curing, like concrete does, what is the surface area? What forces act on the structure and how can the forces be calculated? Calculus is a helpful tool in answering these questions.

Observations

A common design used in the construction of dams is the arch dam. An arch dam is usually built in a narrow canyon and curves toward the water it contains. The canyon itself is used to support the dam. The force of the water against the dam is transferred outward to the canyon walls.

Purpose

In this lab, you will analyze the construction of an arch dam and find its surface area and volume. You will also study the fluid force on one of the dam's gates. You will use *Derive* to verify your results.

References

For more information about the calculus of dam design, see *Calculus, Understanding Change*, a three-part, half-hour video produced by COMAP and funded by the National Science Foundation.

O
ne model for a cross section of an arch dam whose dimensions are given in feet is as follows.

$$f(x) = \begin{cases} 0.03x^2 + 7.1x + 350, & -70 \leq x \leq -16 \\ 389, & -16 < x < 0 \\ -6.593x + 389, & 0 \leq x \leq 59 \end{cases}$$

A graph of the cross section is given below.

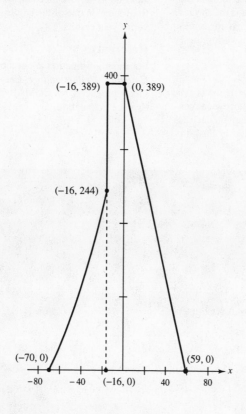

The graph of a cross section of the arch dam is stored in the *Derive* file called LAB0601.MTH. The instructions for this *Derive* file are stored in the text file called LAB0601.TXT.

Name _____

Date _____ Class _____

Instructor _____

1. *Calculating Area Without Calculus.*   Explain how you would calculate the area of a cross section of the arch dam without using Calculus. Use your explanation to calculate the area of a cross section of the arch dam. Is the area you found exact? Why or why not?

_____
_____
_____
_____
_____
_____
_____
_____
_____
_____
_____

2. *Calculating Area With Calculus.*   Explain how you would calculate the area of a cross section of the arch dam using Calculus. Use your explanation to calculate the area of a cross section of the arch dam. Is the area you found exact? Why or why not?

_____
_____
_____
_____
_____
_____
_____
_____
_____

3. ***Calculating Area With Derive.***   Use *Derive* to calculate the area of a cross section of the arch dam. Is the value for area you found using *Derive* the same as the value you found in Exercise 2? If the values are not the same, explain why they are different.

_____

_____

_____

_____

_____

_____

4. ***Calculating Volume.***   To form an arch dam, the cross section described in this lab's Data is swung through an arc, rotating it about the *y*-axis as shown in the figure below. The cross section is rotated 150° and the axis of rotation is 150 feet. Explain how you would calculate the volume of the arch dam. Use your explanation to calculate the volume of the arch dam.

_____

_____

_____

_____

_____

_____

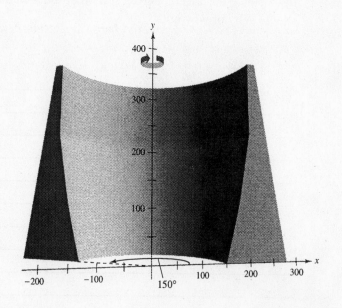

5. *Calculating Volume With Derive.* Use *Derive* to calculate the volume of the arch dam. Is the volume you found using *Derive* the same as the volume you found in Exercise 4? If the values are not the same, explain why they are different.

_____

_____

_____

_____

_____

_____

_____

_____

_____

_____

_____

_____

_____

_____

_____

_____

_____

Fluid Force on a Gate. **Use the following information to answer Exercises 6-9.** A series of vertical gates allows water from the dam to flow to an electrical plant. Each gate has an elliptical shape. So a gate can be properly designed, it is important to determine the fluid force that will be applied to the gate. The force F exerted by a fluid of constant weight-density w (per unit of volume) against a submerged vertical plane region from $y = c$ to $y = d$ is

$$F = w \int_c^d h(y)L(y)dy$$

where $h(y)$ is the depth of the fluid at y and $L(y)$ is the horizontal length of the region at y. The top of the gate is 140 feet above the base of the dam, and the bottom of the gate is 112 feet above the base of the dam. The width of the gate at its center is 16 feet.

6. Find the equation of the ellipse that describes the face of the gate. Assume that the origin of the coordinate system is located at the center of the gate. Use the equation of the ellipse

$$\frac{x^2}{b^2} + \frac{y^2}{a^2} = 1$$

to find the horizontal length $L(y)$ of the region at y.

7. Find the equation that describes the depth $h(y)$ of the water at y. Assume that the origin of the coordinate system is located at the center of the gate and the water can reach the full height of the dam.

8. Find the integral for the fluid force on the gate. Assume the weight-density w of the water is 62.4 pounds per cubic foot. Evaluate the integral. In what unit of measure is the answer?

9. The gate is rotated 90°, so that the top of the gate is 134 feet above the base of the dam, and the bottom of the gate is 118 feet above the base of the dam. The width of the gate at its center is 28 feet. Will the pressure be more than, the same as, or less than the pressure you found in Exercise 8? Explain.

_____

_____

_____

_____

_____

_____

STRETCHING A SPRING
Hooke's Law

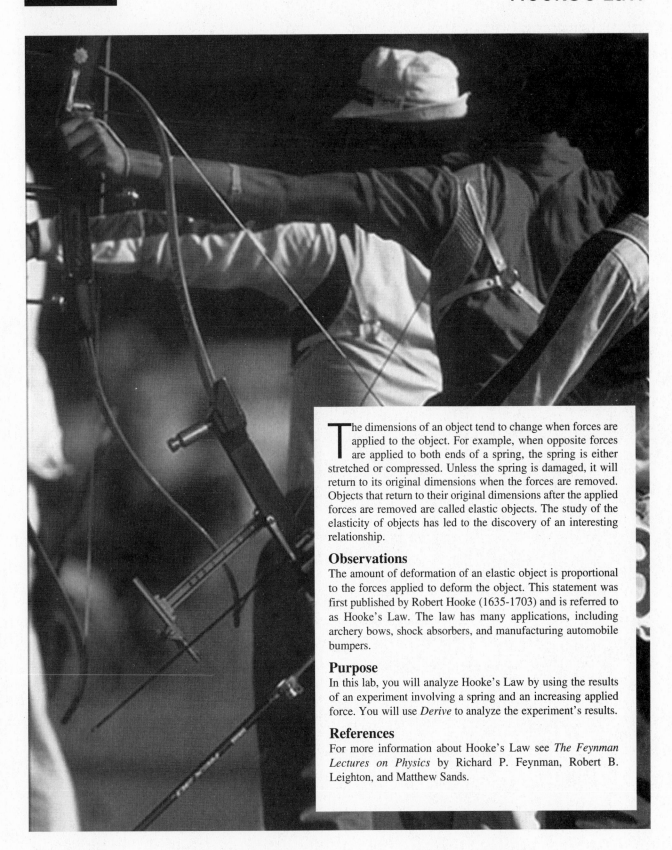

The dimensions of an object tend to change when forces are applied to the object. For example, when opposite forces are applied to both ends of a spring, the spring is either stretched or compressed. Unless the spring is damaged, it will return to its original dimensions when the forces are removed. Objects that return to their original dimensions after the applied forces are removed are called elastic objects. The study of the elasticity of objects has led to the discovery of an interesting relationship.

Observations
The amount of deformation of an elastic object is proportional to the forces applied to deform the object. This statement was first published by Robert Hooke (1635-1703) and is referred to as Hooke's Law. The law has many applications, including archery bows, shock absorbers, and manufacturing automobile bumpers.

Purpose
In this lab, you will analyze Hooke's Law by using the results of an experiment involving a spring and an increasing applied force. You will use *Derive* to analyze the experiment's results.

References
For more information about Hooke's Law see *The Feynman Lectures on Physics* by Richard P. Feynman, Robert B. Leighton, and Matthew Sands.

A force F is applied to a spring and the distance x of the spring is recorded. F is measured in newtons and x is measured in meters. The results of the experiment are shown in the table below.

Distance, x	0.00	0.20	0.39	0.59	0.78	0.98	1.08
Force, F	0.00	3.22	6.61	9.69	13.21	16.38	18.01

Distance, x	1.18	1.27	1.37
Force, F	19.70	21.32	22.73

A scatter plot of the data is given below.

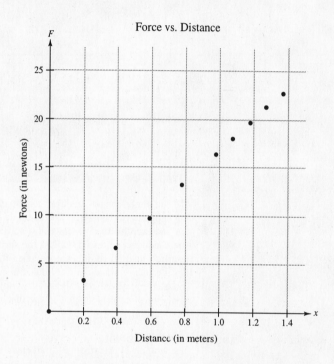

The data in the table and the scatter plot are stored in the *Derive* file called LAB0602.MTH. The instructions for this *Derive* file are stored in the text file called LAB0602.TXT.

Name _____

Date _____ Class _____

Instructor _____

1. **Representing Hooke's Law Mathematically.**   Let F be the force required to stretch or compress an object (within its elastic limits) and let x be the distance that the object is stretched or compressed from its original length. Then Hooke's Law can be represented mathematically by

   $$F = kx$$

   where k is a constant of proportionality. Verbally describe the graph of this equation. What does k represent in the graph of this equation?

   _____

   _____

   _____

   _____

   _____

   _____

   _____

   _____

2. **Calculating the Constant of Proportionality.** Explain how you would calculate the value of k in the formula $F = kx$ using the data from the spring experiment as described in this lab's Data. Then calculate the value of k. Use *Derive* to graph $F = kx$ and the data points. Is the model a good fit to the data? Why or why not? If the model is not a good fit, refine your method for calculating the value of k to obtain a model that is a good fit to the data.

   _____

   _____

   _____

   _____

   _____

   _____

   _____

   _____

3. *Is it Unique?* Do you think the value of k that you found in Exercise 2 can be used for other springs? Why or why not?

_____

_____

_____

_____

_____

4. *Exceeding the Elastic Limit.* Hooke's Law says that if an object is within its elastic limits, the force F required to stretch or compress an object is proportional to the distance x that the object is stretched or compressed from its original length. What do you think would happen if a force was applied to the spring sufficient to stretch the spring beyond its elastic limit? Would the relationship between F and x still be linear?

_____

_____

_____

_____

_____

5. *Work.* If an object is moved along a straight line by a continuously varying force F, then the work W done by the force as the object is moved from $x = a$ to $x = b$ is

$$W = \int_a^b F dx.$$

Rewrite this integral using the force equation you found in Exercise 2. What do you think the graph of W looks like? Describe the relationship between work done to stretch the spring and the distance x the spring is stretched. Is the relationship constant, linear, or quadratic? Explain your reasoning.

_____

_____

_____

_____

_____

_____

6. *Calculating Work.* In Exercise 5 you found an integral for the work done in stretching the spring described in this lab's Data. Complete the table by evaluating this integral using *Derive* and the following distances from the spring's original length. Sketch a graph showing distance on the horizontal axis and work on the vertical axis. Does the graph confirm your answer to Exercise 5? If not, how would you answer Exercise 5 now?

Distance (in meters)	Work
3	
6	
9	
12	
15	

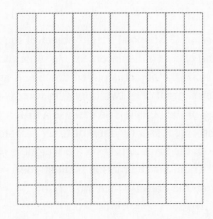

_____

_____

_____

_____

_____

_____

_____

_____

_____

_____

7. **Calculating Additional Work.** Determine the work done when a force of 0.20 newton stretches the spring described in this lab's Data to a length of 3.22 meters. Should the work done in stretching the spring from $x = 3.22$ meters to $x = 6.44$ meters be more than, the same as, or less than this? Explain.

_____

_____

_____

_____

_____

8. **Spring in Motion.** Suppose a rigid object of mass m is attached to the end of a spring and causes a displacement. Assume the spring's mass is negligible compared to m. If the object is pulled down and released, then the resulting oscillations are a product of two opposing forces—the spring force $F = kx$ and the weight mg of the object. You can use a differential equation to find the position of the object as a function of time. According to Newton's Second Law of Motion, the force acting on the weight is ma, where $a = d^2x/dt^2$ is the acceleration. Assuming the motion is undamped—that is, that there are no other forces acting on the object—then $m(d^2x/dt^2) = -kx$ and you have

$$\frac{d^2x}{dt^2} + \frac{k}{m}x = 0.$$

Now suppose a force of 16.59 newtons stretches a spring 1 meter from its natural length. The spring is then stretched an additional 5 meters and released with an initial velocity of 7 meters per second. Use _Derive_ to solve the differential equation and graph its solution. Describe the motion of the spring as the time t increases.

_____

_____

_____

_____

_____

_____

_____

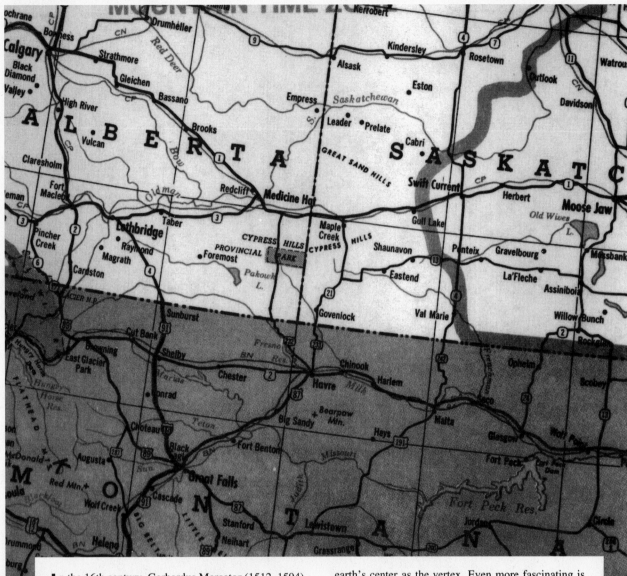

In the 16th century, Gerhardus Mercator (1512–1594) designed a map unlike any other standard flat map. While a constant bearing of 45° is a curved line on a standard flat map, it is a straight line on a Mercator map. Also, angles measured on a Mercator map are the same as angles measured on the globe. These facts make a Mercator map an excellent navigational aid.

Observations

Designing a Mercator map involves projective geometry, but it also involves calculus. To construct the map so that angles between latitude and longitude are preserved, one must evaluate an integral involving the angle formed by the latitude and the equator, with the earth's center as the vertex. Even more fascinating is the fact that Mercator evaluated this integral a century before a formal calculus was developed.

Purpose

In this lab, you will analyze the construction of a Mercator map and the integral used to construct it. You will use *Derive* to analyze the integral.

References

For more information about Mercator maps see the article "Mercator's World Map and the Calculus" by Philip M. Tuchinsky in *UMAP Module 206*.

For lines to appear as straight lines on a flat map, Mercator realized that latitude lines must be stretched horizontally by a scaling factor of sec ϕ, where ϕ is the angle (in radians) of the latitude line. In order for the map to preserve the angles between latitude and longitude lines, the vertical lengths of longitude lines must also be stretched by a scaling factor of sec ϕ at latitude ϕ.

To calculate these vertical lengths, imagine a globe with latitude lines marked at angles of every $\Delta\phi$ radians, with $\Delta\phi = \phi_i - \phi_{i-1}$. The arc length of consecutive latitude lines is $R\Delta\phi$. Therefore, the vertical distance between the first latitude line and the equator is $R\Delta\phi \sec \phi_1$. The vertical distance between the second latitude line and the first latitude line is $R\Delta\phi \sec \phi_2$, and so on, as shown below.

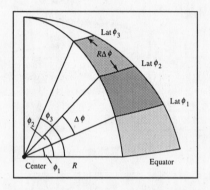
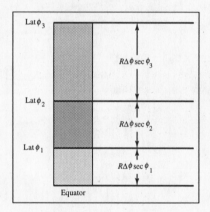

On a globe, the angle between consecutive latitude lines is $\Delta\phi$, and the arc length between them is $R\Delta\phi$ (see the figure on the left above). Therefore, the vertical distance between latitude line i and latitude line $i - 1$ is $R\Delta\phi \sec \phi_i$, and the distance from the equator to the ith latitude line is approximately

$$R\Delta\phi \sec \phi_1 + R\Delta\phi \sec \phi_2 + \cdots + R\Delta\phi \sec \phi_i.$$

The *Derive* file corresponding to this lab is called LAB0701.MTH. The instructions for this *Derive* file are stored in the text file called LAB0701.TXT.

Exercises

Name _____

Date _____ Class _____

Instructor _____

1. **Using Summation Notation and Calculus.**   Use summation notation to write how far from the equator to draw the line representing latitude ϕ_n. As the value for $\Delta\phi$ gets smaller and smaller, the approximations of the distance from the equator to a latitude line get better and better. Use this observation and your knowledge of calculus to calculate the total vertical distance of each latitude line from the equator. Use the result to complete the following table. (Use a globe radius of $R = 6$ inches.)

Latitude Line (in degrees north of the equator)	Distance From Equator
15°	
30°	
45°	
60°	
75°	
90°	

2. Bad Latitude? In Exercise 1, what problem do you encounter when you attempt to calculate the distance from the equator to the latitude line 90° north of the equator? What does this latitude represent on the map?

_____

_____

_____

_____

_____

_____

_____

3. Proof. In the calculation of the total vertical distance of a latitude line from the equator on a Mercator map, you need to evaluate the integral

$$\int \sec \phi \, d\phi.$$

Prove that the following integration formula is true.

$$\int \sec \phi \, d\phi = \ln|\sec \phi + \tan \phi| + C$$

4. Integrating With Technology. Use _Derive_ to evaluate

$$\int \sec \phi \, d\phi.$$

Does the result given by _Derive_ agree with the formula given in Exercise 3? If not, are the two results equivalent? Explain.

_____

_____

_____

_____

_____

_____

5. Are the Results Valid?   In Exercise 3, you showed that

$$\int \sec \phi \, d\phi = \ln|\sec \phi + \tan \phi| + C.$$

Use differentiation to show that the following results are also valid.

(a) $\displaystyle\int \sec \phi \, d\phi = -\ln\left|\tan\left[\frac{1}{2}\left(\frac{\pi}{2} - \phi\right)\right]\right| + C$

(b) $\displaystyle\int \sec \phi \, d\phi = \ln\left|\tan\left[\frac{1}{2}\left(\frac{\pi}{2} + \phi\right)\right]\right| + C$

6. Radians to Degrees.   The angle ϕ for the integral

$$\int \sec \phi \, d\phi$$

is measured in radians. How would you write the integral if the angle ϕ is measured in degrees? Evaluate the indefinite integral and compare the result to those of Exercise 5.

7. The Same Distance?   On a Mercator map, does one inch along the latitude at 30° north of the equator represent the same earth-distance as one inch along the latitude at 60° north of the equator? Explain your reasoning.

_____

_____

_____

_____

_____

_____

_____

8. *Area and Distance.* You know a Mercator map is useful as a navigational aid, but can you use a Mercator map to compare the areas of two regions? Use the Mercator map and the table of areas to answer the question. What happens to the area of a region as you move farther from the equator? Do you think it would be easy to determine distance between two cities on a Mercator map? Explain your reasoning.
(Source: The Universal Almanac)

Region	Area (in square miles)
Africa	11,687,188
Antarctica	5,100,023
Asia	17,176,102
Australia	3,035,651
Europe	4,065,945
North America	9,357,294
South America	6,880,638

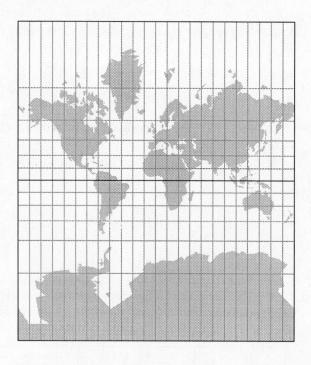

_____

_____

_____

_____

_____

_____

KOCH SNOWFLAKE
Fractals

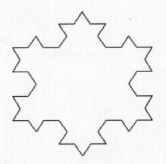

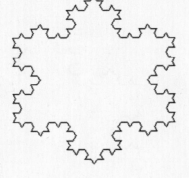

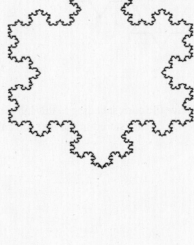

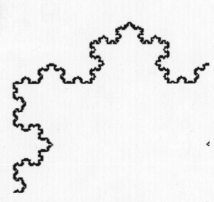

C louds, biological growth, and coastlines are examples of real-life phenomena that seem too complex to be described using typical mathematical functions or relationships. By developing fractal geometry, Benoit Mandelbrot (1924–) found a way to describe real-life phenomena using a new mathematical construct.

Observations

Mandelbrot first used the word fractal in 1975 to describe any geometric object whose detail is not lost as it is magnified. Being "endlessly magnifiable" means that you can zoom in on any portion of the fractal and it will be identical to the original fractal.

Purpose

In this lab, you will analyze some fractals. You will use *Derive* to "zoom in" on different parts of a fractal.

References

For more information about fractals see *The Fractal Geometry of Nature* by Benoit Mandelbrot.

One of the "classic" fractals is the Koch snowflake, named after Swedish mathematician Helge von Koch (1870–1924). The construction of the Koch snowflake begins with an equilateral triangle whose sides are one unit long. In the first iteration, a triangle with sides one-third unit long is added in the center of each side of the original. In the second iteration, a triangle with sides one-ninth unit long is added in the center of each side of the first iteration. Successive iterations continue this process indefinitely. The first four stages are shown below.

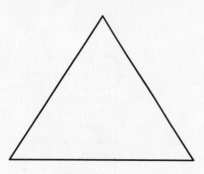

Stage 0

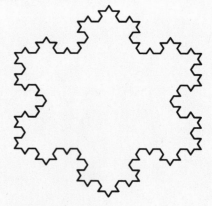

Stage 1

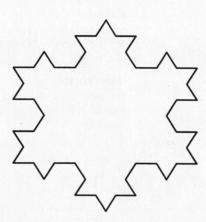

Stage 2

Stage 3

The *Derive* file corresponding to this lab is called LAB0801.MTH. The instructions for this *Derive* file are stored in the text file called LAB0801.TXT.

Name _____

Date _____ Class _____

Instructor _____

1. *Complete the Table.* Use the iteration for the Koch snowflake as described in this lab's Data to complete the following table.

Stage	Sides	Perimeter	Area
0	3	3	$\dfrac{\sqrt{3}}{4}$
1	12	4	$\dfrac{\sqrt{3}}{3}$
2			
3			
4			
5			

$\vdots$

n			

2. *Perimeter and Area.* Using the results of Exercise 1, do you think it's possible for a closed region in the plane to have a finite area and an infinite perimeter? Explain your reasoning.

_____

_____

_____

_____

_____

_____

_____

3. *Start with a Square.* A variation of the Koch snowflake is shown below. This time, the construction begins with a square whose sides are one unit long. In the first iteration, a triangle with sides one-third unit long is added in the center of each side of the square. In the second iteration, a triangle with sides one-ninth unit long is added in the center of each side. Successive iterations continue this process indefinitely. The first four stages are shown below.

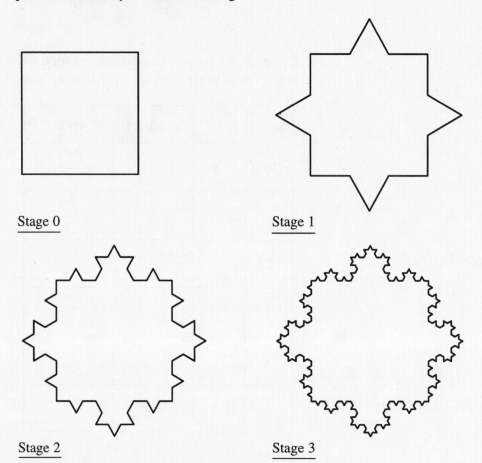

Stage 0   Stage 1

Stage 2   Stage 3

Stage	Sides	Perimeter	Area
0	4	4	1
1	16	$\dfrac{16}{3}$	$1 + \dfrac{\sqrt{3}}{9}$
2			
3			
4			
5			

$\vdots$

n			

4. Start with a Pentagon. Another variation of the Koch snowflake is shown below. This time, the construction begins with a pentagon whose sides are one unit long. In the first iteration, a triangle with sides one-third unit long is added in the center of each side of the pentagon. In the second iteration, a triangle with sides one-ninth unit long is added in the center of each side. Successive iterations continue this process indefinitely. The first four stages are shown below.

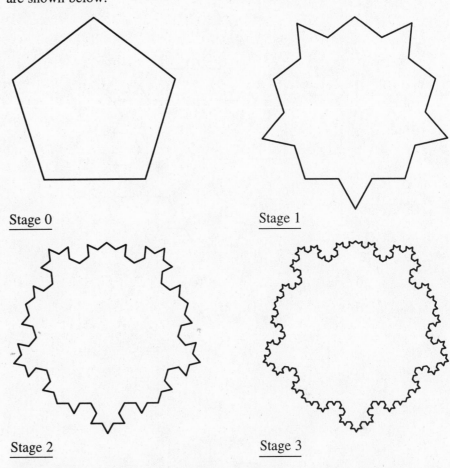

Stage 0

Stage 1

Stage 2

Stage 3

How many sides will the nth iteration have? Do you think the Koch snowflake described in this exercise will have an area equal to, greater than, or smaller than the area of the Koch snowflake described in Exercise 1? Do you think its area will be equal to, greater than, or smaller than the area of the Koch snowflake described in Exercise 3? Explain your reasoning.

_____

_____

5. Comparing Perimeters. Do you think the Koch snowflake described in Exercise 4 will have a perimeter equal to, greater than, or smaller than the perimeter of the Koch snowflake described in Exercise 1? Do you think its perimeter will be equal to, greater than, or smaller than the perimeter of the Koch snowflake described in Exercise 3? Explain your reasoning.

_____

_____

6. *A Koch Curve Using Derive.* *Derive* was used to generate the following graphs of a Koch curve. Use *Derive* to reproduce each graph and record the viewing window you used. Can you find more than one viewing window that reproduces each graph below? If so, list the viewing window values *xmin, xmax, ymin,* and *ymax* you used for each graph.

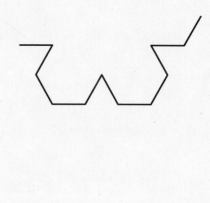

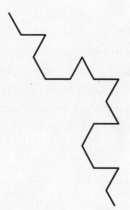

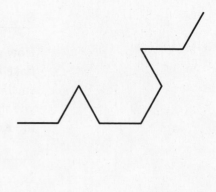

For a tennis ball brand to be approved for tournament play by the United States Tennis Association (USTA), it must satisfy several specifications. One specification is that when the ball is dropped onto a concrete surface from a height of 100 inches, the ball must bounce upward at least 53 inches but no more than 58 inches.

Observations

When a tennis ball is dropped from rest and bounces continuously on a level, concrete surface, each rebound height of the ball is less than any previous height. The total vertical distance the tennis ball travels can be found by calculating the sum of a converging infinite geometric series.

Purpose

In this lab, you will analyze a bouncing tennis ball. You will use an infinite series to measure the total vertical distance traveled by the bouncing tennis ball. You will use *Derive* to calculate the sum of an infinite series.

References

For more information about the physics of a tennis ball see *The Physics of Sports* from the American Institute of Physics.

Oe tennis ball that meets USTA specifications was dropped from a height of 100 inches onto a level, concrete surface. The height of the ball when it reached its apex after a bounce was recorded in the following table.

Number of bounces	0	1	2	3	4	5	6	7	8	9
Height (in inches)	100	55	30.25	16.64	9.15	5.03	2.77	1.52	0.84	0.46

A scatter plot of the data is given below.

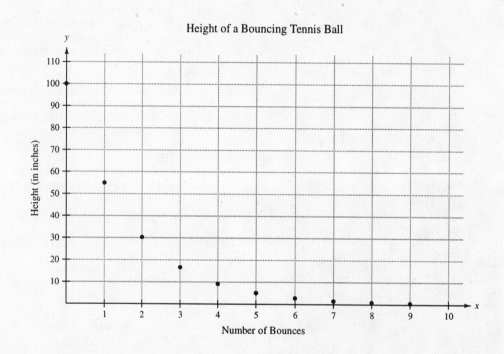

Height of a Bouncing Tennis Ball

The data in the table and the scatter plot are stored in the *Derive* file called LAB0802.MTH. The instructions for this *Derive* file are stored in the text file called LAB0802.TXT.

Name _____

Date _____ Class _____

Instructor _____

1. *Modeling the Data.* What type of mathematical model do you think fits the bouncing tennis ball data? Explain. Apply your model to the bouncing tennis ball data. Then graph the model on the scatter plot below.

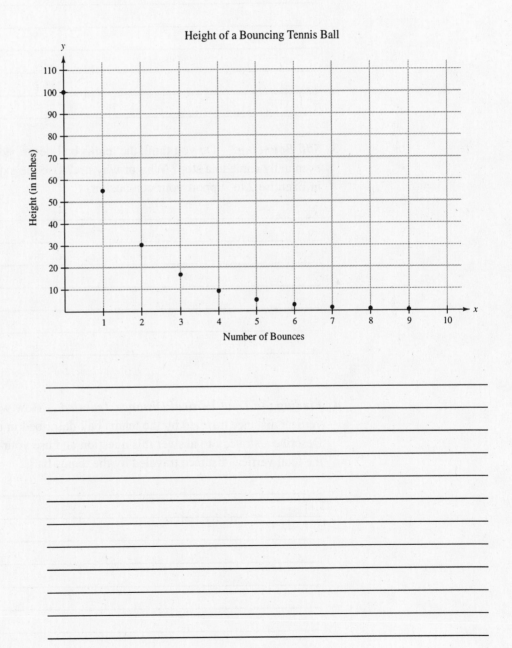

Height of a Bouncing Tennis Ball

_____

_____

_____

_____

_____

_____

_____

_____

_____

_____

_____

_____

2. *Modeling the Data With Derive.* An exponential equation is used in this lab's *Derive* file to model the bouncing tennis ball data. The equation is given by

$$y = y_0 p^n,$$

where y is the rebound height, y_0 is the initial height, p is the rebound rate, and n is the number of bounces. What value is used for y_0? What value is used for p? Explain how the value of p was determined. Compare this model to the one you used in Exercise 1. Is one model better than the other? Why or why not?

_____

_____

_____

_____

_____

_____

_____

3. *Still Bouncing?* Do you think the tennis ball described in this lab's Data eventually came to a stop? Why or why not? Use the exponential model given in Exercise 2 to support your conclusion.

_____

_____

_____

_____

_____

_____

_____

4. *Finding the Total Vertical Distance Traveled.* How would you find the total vertical distance traveled by the tennis ball described in this lab's Data? Describe a strategy to answer this question and use your strategy to determine the total vertical distance traveled by the tennis ball.

_____

_____

_____

_____

_____

_____

5. *Using a Geometric Series.* A geometric series can be used to find the total vertical distance traveled by the tennis ball described in this lab's Data. The total vertical distance traveled is given by

$$D = D_0 + 2\sum_{n=1}^{\infty} D_0 p^n$$

where D is the total vertical distance, D_0 is the initial height, p is the rebound rate, and n is the number of bounces. How does this method of finding the total vertical distance traveled by the tennis ball compare to the one you used in Exercise 4? Let $D_0 = 100$ and $p = 0.55$ and calculate the value of D. Did you obtain the same answer as you did in Exercise 4? If not, explain why the answers are different.

_____

_____

_____

_____

_____

_____

6. *Why Multiply by Two?* Explain why the geometric series

$$2\sum_{n=1}^{\infty} D_0 p^n$$

is multiplied by 2 in the equation for D from Exercise 5.

_____

_____

_____

_____

_____

_____

7. *A Legal Ball?* A tennis ball was dropped from a height of 100 inches onto a level, concrete surface. After five bounces, the tennis ball had traveled a vertical distance of 376 inches. Is this a USTA sanctioned tennis ball? Explain how you determined your answer.

_____

_____

_____

_____

_____

_____

8. *Minimum and Maximum Distances.*   What is the minimum total vertical distance a USTA sanctioned tennis ball could travel if the tennis ball is dropped from a height of 100 inches onto a level, concrete surface? Under the same conditions, what is the greatest total vertical distance a USTA sanctioned tennis ball could travel?

_____

_____

_____

_____

_____

_____

_____

_____

_____

_____

_____

_____

9. *Changing the Initial Height.*   The tennis ball described in this lab's Data is dropped onto a level, concrete surface again, this time from a height of 200 inches. The total vertical distance D traveled by the tennis ball has changed by what factor? Each time you multiply the initial height by a positive integer k, by what factor will you change D?

_____

_____

_____

_____

_____

_____

_____

_____

_____

_____

_____

_____

LAB 9.1

With its high rate of activity and the ability to be seen by the naked-eye, Comet C/1995 O1 (Hale-Bopp), also referred to as Comet Hale-Bopp, was the cause of much excitement in early 1997. Discovered by Alan Hale and Thomas Bopp on July 23, 1995, it has been estimated that Comet Hale-Bopp last passed through the inner solar system over 4000 years ago.

Observations

The study of the orbits of Comet Hale-Bopp and other comets in our solar system leads to an interesting application of conics. The center of the sun is a focus of each orbit, and each orbit has a vertex at the point at which the comet is closest to the sun. Unlike comets with elliptical orbits, comets with parabolic or hyperbolic orbits pass through our solar system only once.

Purpose

In this lab, you will analyze the orbits of several comets and determine an equation for their orbits using rectangular and polar equations. You will use *Derive* to graph the equations of the orbits.

References

For more information about comets (plus asteroids and planets) see *Exploring Planetary Worlds* by David Morrison. Astronomical data about Comet Hale-Bopp courtesy of Daniel W. E. Green, Associate Director, Central Bureau for Astronomical Telegrams.

Comet Hale-Bopp has an elliptical orbit with an eccentricity of $e \approx 0.995$. Comet Hale-Bopp's perihelion distance (the shortest distance to the sun) in 1997 was 0.914 astronomical unit (AU). (An astronomical unit is defined to be the mean distance between the earth and the sun, 92.956×10^6 million miles or 1.496×10^{11} meters.) A graphical representation of Comet Hale-Bopp's orbit is given below.

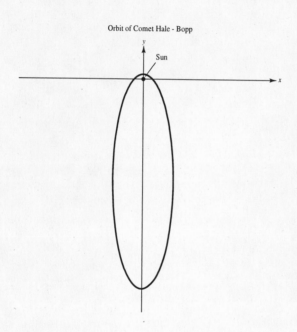

Orbit of Comet Hale - Bopp

The *Derive* file corresponding to this lab is called LAB0901.MTH. The instructions for this *Derive* file are stored in the text file called LAB0901.TXT.

Name _____

Date _____ Class _____

Instructor _____

1. **Finding a Polar Equation.** Find a polar equation for Comet Hale-Bopp's orbit. Use an equation of the form

$$r = \frac{ed}{1 + e \sin \theta}$$

where e is the eccentricity and $|d|$ is the distance between the focus at the pole and its corresponding directrix. Use the equation to find Comet Hale-Bopp's aphelion distance (farthest distance from the sun). What value of θ corresponds to the aphelion distance? Explain your reasoning.

_____

_____

_____

_____

_____

_____

_____

_____

_____

_____

_____

_____

2. Graphing a Polar Equation. Use *Derive* to graph the equation you found in Exercise 1 with θ varying from $\pi/2$ to $3\pi/2$. Then graph the equation again with θ varying from $\pi/2$ to $5\pi/2$, and again with θ varying from $\pi/2$ to $9\pi/2$. What do you observe?

_____

_____

_____

_____

_____

_____

3. A Set of Parametric Equations. Find a set of parametric equations for Comet Hale-Bopp's orbit with the sun at the origin. Use equations of the form

$$x = b \cos \theta + h \text{ and } y = a \sin \theta + k$$

where a is half of the length of the major axis, b is half of the length of the minor axis, and (h, k) is the center of the ellipse. Use *Derive* to graph the equations. Repeat Exercise 2 using the set of parametric equations and compare each graph to the corresponding polar graph.

_____

_____

_____

_____

_____

4. Using a Rectangular Coordinate System. Find a rectangular equation for Comet Hale-Bopp's orbit. Use an equation of the form

$$\frac{x^2}{b^2} + \frac{y^2}{a^2} = 1.$$

(Note: Unlike the equations you found in Exercises 1 and 3, this equation does not place the sun at the origin.) Use *Derive* to graph the equation. Of the three different ways you have represented Comet Hale-Bopp's orbit in this lab, which way would you choose to represent the orbit? Explain your reasoning.

_____

_____

_____

_____

_____

5. *Determining the Type of Orbit.* The type of orbit for a comet can be determined as follows.

Ellipse: $\quad v < \sqrt{\dfrac{2GM}{p}}$

Parabola: $\quad v = \sqrt{\dfrac{2GM}{p}}$

Hyperbola: $\quad v > \sqrt{\dfrac{2GM}{p}}$

In these three formulas, v is the velocity of the comet at the vertex (in meters per second), G is the gravitational constant where $G \approx 6.67 \times 10^{-11}$ cubic meters per kilogram-second squared, M is the mass of the sun where $M \approx 1.991 \times 10^{30}$ kilograms, and p is the distance between one vertex and one focus of the comet's orbit (in meters). Determine the value of

$$\sqrt{\dfrac{2GM}{p}}$$

for Comet Hale-Bopp. Show that the orbit of Comet Hale-Bopp is an ellipse if it was traveling at about 44 km/sec or less when it reached perihelion. If p is held constant, find a velocity at the perihelion that would mean Comet Hale-Bopp has a parabolic orbit. For what velocities at the perihelion would Comet Hale-Bopp have a hyperbolic orbit if p is held constant?

_____

_____

_____

_____

_____

_____

_____

_____

_____

_____

_____

_____

_____

6. *Orbital Period of Comet Hale-Bopp.* Estimates of Comet Hale-Bopp's orbit indicate that it last passed the earth around 2214 B.C (about 4210 years ago) and it will return around 4377 A.D. (about 2380 years from now). List several factors that could be changing the orbital period of Comet Hale-Bopp.

_____

_____

_____

_____

_____

_____

7. *Applying Kepler's Second Law to Comet Hale-Bopp.* Kepler's Second Law states that as a planet moves about the sun, a ray from the sun to the planet sweeps out equal areas in equal times. This law can also be applied to comets (or other heavenly bodies) with elliptical orbits. Applying Kepler's Second Law to Comet Hale-Bopp, what conclusion can you make about the comet's velocity as it approaches perihelion distance? What conclusion can you make about the comet's velocity as it approaches aphelion?

_____

_____

_____

_____

_____

_____

8. *Verifying Kepler's Second Law.* The length of time for Comet Hale-Bopp to move in its orbit from $\theta = \alpha$ to $\theta = \beta$ is given by

$$\frac{t}{2380} = \frac{\text{Area of Segment}}{\text{Area of Ellipse}} = \frac{\frac{1}{2}\int_{\alpha}^{\beta} r^2 \, d\theta}{\pi ab}$$

where t is the time in years. Use *Derive* to calculate the number of days t it takes for the comet to move from

$$\theta = \frac{3\pi}{4} \quad \text{to} \quad \theta = \frac{5\pi}{4}.$$

_____

_____

_____

_____

Cables have been used in the design of many different types of structures. They have been used in the design of suspension bridges such as New York's Verrazano Narrows Bridge, and in the design of hanging power lines, guy wires, and other constructs. While each design uses a cable structure, the way the cable structures are implemented can be different.

Observations

The graphs of the main cables for a suspension bridge are different than the graphs of the cables for hanging power lines. The graphs of the main cables for a suspension bridge are parabolas, and the graphs of the cables for hanging power lines are catenaries. One reason the graphs are different is because of the way the cables distribute weight.

Purpose

In this lab, you will analyze the cable structure of a suspension bridge. You will use *Derive* to graph a cable structure and to find arc length.

References

For more information about cable structures see *Cable Structures* by Max Irvine.

Suspension bridges are stable when the horizontal and vertical forces acting on its main cables are in equilibrium. This equilibrium occurs when the main cables are in the shape of parabolas.

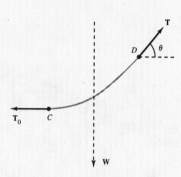

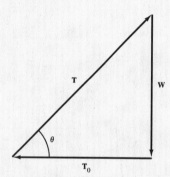

The forces acting on the main cable are shown in the diagram above as directed line segments, indicating both the magnitude and the direction of the forces. At the center of the cable, the tension force T_0 is horizontal. T is the tension at point D, and is directed along the tangent at point D. The uniformly distributed load supported by the section CD of the cable is represented by W.

The *Derive* file corresponding to this lab is called LAB1001.MTH. The instructions for this *Derive* file are stored in the text file called LAB1001.TXT.

Name _____

Date _____ Class _____

Instructor _____

1. *Finding a Parabolic Equation.*   When the Verrazano Narrows Bridge opened in 1964, it was the world's largest suspension bridge. The bridge's main cable is suspended from towers 693 feet above the roadway at either end of a 4260-foot span. The low point in the center of the cable is 303 feet above the roadway. Given that the cable hangs in the shape of a parabola, find a rectangular equation of the form

$$(x - h)^2 = 4p(y - k)$$

describing the shape of the cable. To determine the equation, where did you place the origin of the coordinate axes?

_____

_____

_____

_____

_____

2. *Another Parabolic Equation.*   The equation that describes the shape of a suspension bridge's cable is given by

$$y = \frac{wx^2}{2\|T_0\|}$$

where w is the load per unit length measured horizontally and $\|T_0\|$ is the minimum tension. For a suspension bridge such as the Verrazano Narrows Bridge, the equation describes a parabola centered at the origin with the origin occurring at the lowest point of the cable midway between the two main supports. Use this equation to describe the shape of the main cable if the cable supports a load of $w = 10,800$ pounds per foot and the cable's sag (the vertical distance from the supports to the cable's lowest point) is 390 feet.

_____

_____

_____

_____

3. *Graph the Equations.* Use *Derive* to graph the parabolic equations you found in Exercises 1 and 2 on the same set of axes. (If necessary, rewrite the equation found in Exercise 1 so that the origin is the same as the one used in Exercise 2.) Are the graphs the same? Why or why not?

_____

_____

_____

_____

_____

4. *Arc Length.* Determine the length of Verrazano Narrows Bridge's main cable by evaluating the following integral by hand, where dy/dx is the derivative of either equation found in Exercises 1 and 2.

$$s = 2\int_0^{2130} \sqrt{1 + \left(\frac{dy}{dx}\right)^2}\, dx$$

Evaluate the integral using *Derive* and compare the result to the one you obtained by hand. Compared to the span of the bridge and the lowest point of the cable, does the length of the cable seem reasonable? Why or why not? What is the length of the cable from the cable's lowest point to either support?

_____

_____

_____

_____

_____

5. *Arc Length at Extreme Temperatures.* The extreme temperatures of summer and winter can effect the sag of the main cable. The Verrazano Narrows Bridge was designed with extreme temperatures in mind, and the sag height can vary from 386 feet to 394 feet. Use the equation from Exercise 2 to describe the shape of the cable at each height. Then use *Derive* to find the length of the cable for the minimum and maximum sag heights. During what time of year would you expect the sag height to be 386 feet? During what time of year would you expect the sag height to be 394 feet? Explain your reasoning.

_____

_____

_____

_____

_____

6. *Magnitude of Tension.* The tension at a point (x, y) along the main cable is given by

$$\|\mathbf{T}\| = \sqrt{\|\mathbf{T_0}\| + wx^2}.$$

Substitute the values for $\|\mathbf{T_0}\|$ and w from Exercise 2. Determine the maximum and minimum magnitudes of $\mathbf{T}$ with respect to x. Where on the Verrazano Narrows Bridge does the maximum tension occur? Where on the bridge does the minimum tension occur? Determine the maximum and minimum magnitudes of $\mathbf{T}$ with respect to x when the sag height is 386 feet and 394 feet.

_____

_____

_____

_____

_____

_____

_____

_____

_____

_____

7. *Tension and Tangent Lines.* Find the tangents to the cable at the maximum and minimum values found in Exercise 6. Graph the tangents and the tension $\mathbf{T}$ at these values on the same graph. What do you notice about the tangent and the tension $\mathbf{T}$ at each value? Can you use the tangent line to determine the direction of $\mathbf{T}$? If so, determine the direction of $\mathbf{T}$ at the maximum and minimum values with respect to the horizontal.

_____

_____

_____

_____

_____

_____

_____

_____

_____

8. *Direction of Tension.*   The direction of the tension **T** at D is given by

$$\tan \theta = \frac{wx}{\|\mathbf{T}_0\|}.$$

Use this formula to verify the directions you found in Exercise 7 for **T**.

_____

_____

_____

_____

9. *Supports at Different Elevations.*   Because the suspension towers for the main cable of the Verrazano Narrows Bridge are the same height, the cable's lowest point is midway between the towers. When the heights of the supports for a cable structure are different, the position of the cable's lowest point is *not* midway between the supports. Determine the following for a cable that hangs between a 75-foot high tower and a 125-foot high tower, and supports a uniformly distributed load of 800 pounds per foot. Assume the towers are 1000 feet apart and the lowest point of the cable just touches the roadway.

a. Determine an equation that describes the shape of the cable.

_____

_____

_____

_____

b. Where is the lowest point of the cable? Where is the highest point?

_____

_____

_____

_____

c. How long is the cable? How long is the cable from the lowest point to the highest point?

_____

_____

_____

_____

RACE-CAR CORNERING
Vector-Valued Functions

The Indianapolis Motor Speedway is the host of the internationally famous Indianapolis 500. The speedway has two 3300-foot-long straightaways, two 660-foot-long straightaways, and four 1320-foot-long turns. Not all speedways have this symmetry, and the lack of it can cause variation in the speed and velocity with which a race car can negotiate each turn.

Observations

The Walt Disney World Speedway in Orlando, Florida has three straightaways and three turns. The straightaways have lengths of 1487 feet, 572 feet, and 909 feet. The turns have lengths of 990.35 feet, 976.35 feet, and 417.40 feet.

Purpose

In this lab, you will analyze the turns at Walt Disney World Speedway using vector-valued functions. You will use *Derive* to aid you in your analysis.

References

Information about Indianapolis Motor Speedway and Walt Disney World Speedway courtesy of Kevin Forbes, Director of Engineering & Construction at Indianapolis Motor Speedway.

The position of a certain race car on Turn 1 at Walt Disney World Speedway can be approximated by the following position vector, where t is the time measured in seconds.

$$\mathbf{r}(t) = x(t)\mathbf{i} + y(t)\mathbf{j}$$

$$= 446.85 \cos(0.4759t)\mathbf{i} + 446.85 \sin(0.4759t)\mathbf{j}, \quad 0 < t < 4.66$$

The race car's velocity (comprising both speed and direction) can be represented by a velocity vector. The race car's acceleration (any change in velocity, whether in speed or direction) can be represented by an acceleration vector.

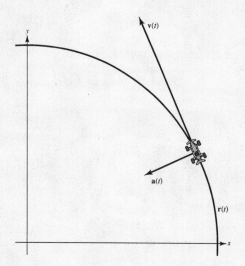

The *Derive* file corresponding to this lab is called LAB1101.MTH. The instructions for this *Derive* file are stored in the text file called LAB1101.TXT.

Name _____

Date _____ Class _____

Instructor _____

1. *Finding Velocity and Acceleration Vectors.* Find the velocity and acceleration vectors for the race car whose position vector is given in this lab's Data. What is the speed of the race car as it moves through the turn? Is the speed of the race car through the turn constant? Is the velocity of the race car constant? What is the acceleration of the race car as it moves through the curve? Is the acceleration vector **a** constant? Explain your reasoning.

_____

_____

_____

_____

_____

_____

_____

2. *Turn 2.* Repeat Exercise 1 for Turn 2, where the position vector is given by

$$\mathbf{r}(t) = 522.47 \cos(0.4211t)\mathbf{i} + 522.47 \sin(0.4211t)\mathbf{j}, \qquad 0 < t < 4.44.$$

_____

_____

_____

_____

_____

_____

_____

3. *Turn 3.* Repeat Exercise 1 for Turn 3, where the position vector is given by

$$\mathbf{r}(t) = 733.89 \cos(0.3797t)\mathbf{i} + 733.89 \sin(0.3797t)\mathbf{j}, \qquad 0 < t < 1.50.$$

_____

_____

_____

_____

_____

_____

4. *Taking Turns.* Use *Derive* to determine the curvature of each turn and record your results below.

Curvature of Turn 1:

Curvature of Turn 2:

Curvature of Turn 3:

Considering each turn's curvature and the race car's velocity vector for each turn, which turn do you think is the "easiest" for the race car to negotiate? Which turn do you think is the "hardest" for the race car to negotiate? Explain your reasoning.

_____

_____

_____

_____

_____

_____

_____

_____

_____

_____

5. ***Make a Table.***   Use the position vector given in this lab's Data to make a table of the race car's positions for several values of t between $t = 0.00$ and $t = 4.66$.

t	0.00	1.00	2.00	3.00	4.00	4.66
$x(t)$						
$y(t)$						

6. ***Graphing Velocity and Acceleration Vectors.***   Plot the results of Exercise 5 on the graph below. At each position, draw the velocity vector and the acceleration vector. What does each velocity vector have in common? What does each acceleration vector have in common?

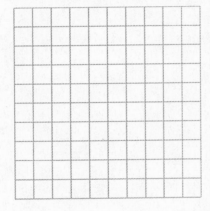

_____

_____

_____

_____

_____

_____

_____

_____

_____

7. *Staying on Track.* Centripetal force is the force required to hold a moving object in a circular path. Centripetal force can be calculated using the formula

$$F = \frac{mv^2}{r}$$

where F is the centripetal force, m is mass (in pounds), v is speed (in feet per second), and r is radius (in feet). Assume the mass of the race car described in this lab's Data is 1800 pounds. Find the centripetal force required in each turn to hold the race car on the track.

Turn 1:

Turn 2:

Turn 3:

PUTTING A SHOT
Projectile Motion

The men's shot put has been a test of strength for centuries. Early versions of the shot were heavy stones. Today's athletes use a shot made of metal weighing 7.26 kilograms (16 pounds). The men's shot put record by the end of 1960 was little more than 20 meters. Twenty eight years later, the record had moved beyond the 23-meter mark.

Observations

The angle of elevation of the shot's release is important to the athlete. If the angle is too steep, too much of the initial velocity will be used to send the shot up and horizontal distance will be sacrificed. If the angle is too low, the shot will not stay above ground long enough to travel very far.

Purpose

In this lab, you will analyze the men's shot put and the effect of different release heights and angles. You will use *Derive* to experimentally find an optimal angle of elevation to maximize the horizontal distance traveled by a shot. You will compare your experimental value with that of estimated angles of elevation used for world record shot puts.

References

For more information about the physics of a shot put, see "Dynamics: Throwing the Javelin, Putting the Shot" by M. S. Klamkin in the *The UMAP Journal* (Vol. VI, No. 2).

Data

The year of a record set in the men's shot put and the record distance in meters is given in the table below. Let x represent the year, where $x = 0$ corresponds to 1900. Let y represent the record distance in meters.

Year, x	60	60	60	60	60	62	64	64
Distance, y	19.38	19.45	19.67	19.99	20.06	20.08	20.10	20.20

Year, x	64	65	67	73	76	76	78	83
Distance, y	20.68	21.52	21.78	21.82	21.85	22.00	22.15	22.22

Year, x	85	86	87	87	87	88	90
Distance, y	22.62	22.64	22.79	22.81	22.91	23.06	23.12

A scatter plot of the data is given below.

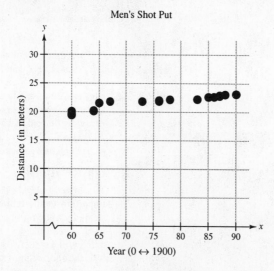

Men's Shot Put

The data in the table and the scatter plot are stored in the *Derive* file called LAB1102.MTH. The instructions for this *Derive* file are stored in the text file called LAB1102.TXT.

Name _____

Date _____ Class _____

Instructor _____

1. *Length of Time in the Air.* Neglecting air resistance, the path of a shot put launched from an initial height h with initial speed v_0 and angle of elevation θ is described by the vector function

$$r(t) = (v_0 \cos \theta)t\mathbf{i} + \left[h + (v_0 \sin \theta)t - \frac{1}{2}gt^2\right]\mathbf{j}$$

where g is the gravitational constant. Show that the length of time t (in seconds) that the shot will remain in the air is given by the following.

$$t = \frac{v_0 \sin \theta + \sqrt{v_0^2 \sin^2 \theta + 2gh}}{g}$$

2. *Horizontal Distance Traveled.* Use the position function given in Exercise 1 to show that the horizontal distance x (in meters) traveled by the shot is given by the following.

$$x = \frac{v_0^2 \cos \theta}{g}\left(\sin \theta + \sqrt{\sin^2 \theta + \frac{2gh}{v_0^2}}\right)$$

3. *The Effect of Initial Height and Initial Speed.* Use the horizontal distance x (in meters) given in Exercise 2 to answer the following.

a. What effect does increasing the initial height h have on the horizontal distance traveled?

_____

_____

_____

_____

_____

_____

_____

_____

b. What effect does increasing the initial speed v_0 have on the horizontal distance traveled?

_____

_____

_____

_____

_____

_____

_____

_____

_____

_____

c. To maximize horizontal distance, should a shot putter try to maximize the initial height, the initial speed, both or neither? Explain your reasoning.

_____

_____

_____

_____

_____

_____

_____

_____

_____

4. *Finding the Optimal Angle Experimentally.* What angle of elevation θ should the shot be released to maximize horizontal distance? Use *Derive* to experiment with different integer values of θ (in degrees) to produce a shot put with maximum horizontal distance if the release height is 2.1 meters and the initial velocity is 13.2 meters per second. What is the value of this angle?

5. *Finding the Optimal Angle Analytically.* The maximum horizontal distance x_{max} and the optimal angle of elevation θ_{max} are related by the following equation.

$$x_{max} = h \tan 2\theta_{max}$$

Use this equation to find the optimal angle for a shot released at a height of 2.1 meters that travels a horizontal distance of 25 meters. Does the value agree with the experimental value you determined in Exercise 4? Why or why not?

_____

_____

_____

_____

_____

6. *Angle of a World Record.* Use the equation given in Exercise 5 to estimate the angle used for the world records given in the table below. (Assume the release height for each record is 2.1 meters.) Compare the angles. Do the angles nearly agree? How do these angles compare to the results of Exercises 4 and 5?

Year	Distance (in meters)	Angle (in degrees)
1983	22.22	
1985	22.62	
1986	22.64	
1987	22.79	
1987	22.81	
1987	22.91	
1988	23.06	
1990	23.12	

_____

_____

_____

_____

_____

7. *Modeling the Data.* An exponential equation was used to model the world records given in this lab's Data. Let x represent the year, where $x = 0$ corresponds to 1900. Let y represent the record distance in meters. The equation for the model is

$$y = 14.76(1.005)^x.$$

Use the model to estimate the world records for the following years. Do you think the model is accurate for all of the years? Why or why not?

Year	Distance (in meters)
2002	
2012	
2022	
2032	
2042	

_____

_____

_____

_____

_____

_____

8. *World Record Angles.* Use the equation given in Exercise 5 to estimate the angle used for the world records you estimated in Exercise 8. (Assume the release height for each record is 2.1 meters.) Compare the angles to those you found in Exercise 6.

Year	Angle (in degrees)
2002	
2012	
2022	
2032	
2042	

_____

_____

_____

_____

_____

_____

Satellite Dishes, Flashlights, and Solar Energy Collectors

Using the Reflective Property of Parabolas

Many objects take advantage of simple, yet powerful, mathematical properties. For example, a parabolic mirror used by a solar energy collector takes advantage of a special property of parabolas. This special property of parabolas is also used in more common objects, such as flashlights and satellite receiving dishes.

Observations

One way to describe the property is to say that *all incoming rays that are parallel to the axis of the parabola reflect directly through the focus of the parabola.* Likewise, *all outgoing rays from the focus that come in contact with the parabola will be reflected parallel to the axis of the parabola.* This property of parabolas is sometimes called the reflective property of parabolas.

Purpose

In this lab, you will analyze the use of parabolas and the reflective property of parabolas in satellite receiving dishes, solar energy collectors and flashlights. You will also analyze the advantages of other geometrical shapes. You will use *Derive* to aid you in your analysis.

References

For more information about the satellite television industry, see "Satellite TV Comes Down to Earth", *Popular Science*, November, 1996.

The shape of a satellite dish is a circular paraboloid. One way to model a circular paraboloid is by using a special case of the elliptic paraboloid formula

$$z = \frac{x^2}{a^2} + \frac{y^2}{b^2}$$

and using $a = b$ to write the formula as

$$z = \frac{x^2}{a^2} + \frac{y^2}{a^2}.$$

For this model, the paraboloid opens up and has its vertex at the origin. For a satellite dish, the axis of the paraboloid should pass through the satellite so that all incoming signals are parallel to the paraboloid's axis. When incoming rays strike the surface of the paraboloid at a point P, they reflect at the same angle as they would if they were reflecting off a plane that was tangent to the surface at point P, as shown in the left-hand figure below.

In the plane, all parabolas have a special reflective property. One way to describe the property is to say that *all incoming rays that are parallel to the axis of the parabola reflect directly through the focus of the parabola*, as shown in the right-hand figure below. In a similar manner, all rays coming into a paraboloid are reflected to the paraboloid's focus.

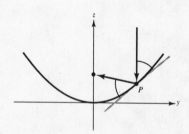

The *Derive* file corresponding to this lab is called LAB1201.MTH. The instructions for this *Derive* file are stored in the text file called LAB1201.TXT.

Name _____

Date _____ Class _____

Instructor _____

1. **Where is the Receiver?**   You are designing a satellite receiving dish. At
   what point should you place the receiver? Explain your reasoning.

   _____

   _____

   _____

   _____

   _____

   _____

   _____

   _____

2. **Find an Equation.**   Determine an equation of the form

$$z = \frac{x^2}{a^2} + \frac{y^2}{a^2}$$

   for a satellite dish that has a radius of 10 feet and a depth of 3.5 feet as
   shown in the figure below.

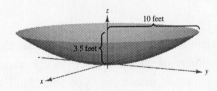

   What is the domain and range of the equation? At what point should you
   place the receiver?

3. *Using a Surface of Revolution.* Imagine that the parabola given by

$$x^2 = 4py$$

is revolved about the y-axis to form a dish of radius r (see figure below).

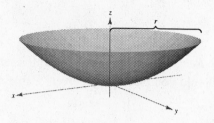

This surface of revolution can be used as a model for a satellite receiving dish. If $p = 5$, then the parabola is

$$x^2 = 20y$$

and has its vertex at the origin and focus at $(0, 5)$. Part of the cost of constructing a receiving dish is related to surface area. Find the surface area of the dish formed by revolving a segment of the parabola $x^2 = 20y$ about the y-axis to form a dish of radius r. The surface area is roughly proportional to the cube of what factor?

4. *Comparing Answers.* Use *Derive* to find the surface area of the dish formed by revolving a segment of the parabola $x^2 = 20y$ about the y-axis to form a dish of radius r. Compare the surface area you found in Exercise 3 to *Derive*'s value and verify that the answers are equivalent. If the answers are not equivalent, explain why they are different.

5. *Using an Elliptic Paraboloid as a Reflector.*   Instead of being used as a receiver like a satellite dish, a flashlight uses an elliptic paraboloid as a reflector. The flashlight's bulb is placed at the focus of a parabolic reflector. A certain flashlight has a reflector that is 8 centimeters wide at the head of the flashlight. The flashlight's bulb is located at the focus of the parabola, 1.5 centimeters from the vertex of the reflector as shown in the figure below.

Find an equation for a cross section of the reflector of the form

$$x^2 = 4py$$

where x and y are measured in centimeters. Determine a segment of the parabola that can be revolved about the y-axis to form the reflector. Find the surface area of the reflector formed by the surface of revolution.

6. *A Parabolic Solar Collector.* The world's largest solar-thermal complex, Luz International, is located in California's Mojave Desert. Parabolic mirrors that look like troughs are used to reflect the sun's rays onto tubes filled with oil. The heated oil is then used to boil water, which sends steam to a turbine. Mechanical drives slowly rotate the mirrors to keep the reflected sunlight focused on the oil-filled tubes.

A cross section of a parabolic mirror used in this type of parabolic solar collector can be modeled by

$$y = \frac{x^2}{25}$$

where x and y are measured in feet. The oil-filled tube is located at the focus of the parabola as shown in the figure below

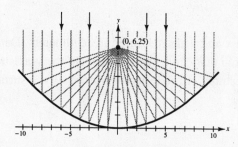

Describe the graph of the collector with respect to three dimensions. If the collector is 18 feet long, determine the surface area of the collector and the equation of the focal line.

_____

_____

_____

_____

_____

_____

_____

HYPERTHERMIA TREATMENTS FOR TUMORS

Volume

H eating malignant tumors to a temperature of about 45°C can cause the tumors to regress. This treatment, known as hyperthermia, uses microwaves to heat the tumors. It is estimated that hyperthermia can increase the effectiveness of radiation and chemotherapy by a factor of two.

Observations

The tumor temperature during treatment is highest at the center and gradually decreases toward the edges. Regions of tissue having the same temperature, called equitherms, can be visualized as closed surfaces that are nested one inside of the other. One of the difficulties in effectively applying the hyperthermia treatment is determining the portion of the tumor heated to an effective temperature.

Purpose

In this lab, you will analyze simple tumor shapes and determine the portion of the tumor that has been heated to an effective temperature. You will use *Derive* to aid you in your analysis.

References

For more information about hyperthermia treatments for tumors see the article "Heat Therapy for Tumors" by Leah Edelstine-Keshet in the Summer, 1991 issue of *The UMAP Journal*.

When normal tissue is heated, it is cooled by the dilation of blood vessels. A tumor has very few interior blood vessels and therefore is unable to take advantage of this cooling process.

The shapes of some tumors can be approximated by spheres or ellipsoids. The equitherms for a spherical tumor and an elliptical tumor are given below. Notice in the graphs that the hottest area is at the tumor's center.

Thermal Patterns Determined by APA Technology

Courtesy of Cheung Laboratories, Inc.

The problem of determining the portion of the tumor that has been heated to an effective temperature reduces to finding the ratio V_T/V, where V is the volume of the entire tumor and V_T is the volume of the portion of the tumor that is heated above temperature T.

The *Derive* file corresponding to this lab is called LAB1301.MTH. The instructions for this *Derive* file are stored in the text file called LAB1301.TXT.

Name _____

Date _____ Class _____

Instructor _____

1. ***A Necessary Measurement?*** Is it necessary to measure the temperature of the tumor's center if you know the temperature of the equitherm at half the radius of the tumor has exceeded the effective temperature? Explain your reasoning.

_____

_____

_____

_____

_____

_____

_____

_____

_____

2. ***Treating a Spherical Tumor.*** When treating a spherical tumor, a probe is used to determine that the temperature has reached an effective level to about one-fourth the radius of the tumor. Determine the value of the ratio V_T/V. Is the value $\frac{1}{4}$? Explain your reasoning. If the radius of the tumor is 2.5 centimeters, what percent of the tumor reached an effective temperature?

_____

_____

_____

_____

_____

_____

_____

_____

_____

3. **Complete the Table.** Complete the table below, where r is the radius of a spherical tumor, V_T is the volume of the portion of the tumor that is heated above temperature T, and V is the volume of the tumor. Describe any patterns you see in the table.

Radius of tumor that has reached an effective temperature	V_T	$\dfrac{V_T}{V}$
$\dfrac{1}{4}r$		
$\dfrac{1}{3}r$		
$\dfrac{1}{2}r$		
$\dfrac{2}{3}r$		
$\dfrac{3}{4}r$		
r		

Use the table above to answer the following questions.

a. When the temperature has reached an effective level equivalent to half the radius of the tumor, is

$$\frac{V_T}{V} = \frac{1}{2}?$$

If not, determine the portion of r that has been heated when $\dfrac{V_T}{V} = \dfrac{1}{2}$.

b. For what heated portion of r is $\dfrac{V_T}{V} = \dfrac{3}{4}$?

4. ***A Tumor Modeled by a Wrinkled Sphere.*** A certain tumor can be modeled by the wrinkled sphere given by the equation

$$\rho = 0.5 + 0.345 \sin 8\theta \sin \phi, \, 0 \leq \theta \leq 2\pi, \, 0 \leq \phi \leq \pi.$$

Explain a strategy for estimating the volume of the wrinkled sphere without using integration. Use your strategy to calculate an estimate.

_____

_____

_____

_____

_____

_____

_____

5. ***Using Integration to Calculate Volume.*** Find the volume of the tumor described in Exercise 4 using integration. How good was your estimate in Exercise 4? What was the percent error of your estimate?

6. *Using Derive to Calculate Volume.* Find the volume of the tumor described in Exercise 4 using *Derive*. Compare the result to Exercise 5. If necessary, show that the results are equivalent. If the results are not equivalent, explain why not.

_____

_____

_____

_____

_____

_____

_____

_____

7. *A Tumor Modeled by a Bumpy Sphere.* A certain tumor can be modeled by the bumpy sphere given by the equation

$$\rho = 0.75 + 0.35 \sin 8\theta \sin 4\phi, \; 0 \le \theta \le 2\pi, 0 \le \phi \le \pi.$$

Find the volume of the tumor using integration.

8. *Using Derive to Calculate Volume.* Find the volume of the tumor described in Exercise 7 using *Derive*. Compare the result to Exercise 7. If necessary, show that the results are equivalent. If the results are not equivalent, explain why not.

_____

_____

_____

_____

_____

_____

_____

_____

Mathematician Helaman Ferguson combines science and art with his unique mathematical sculptures. Ferguson's sculptures are the concrete embodiments of mathematical concepts that incorporate ideas such as series expansions and vector fields into their creation. Some of the basic images in his work are tori and double tori, Möbius strips, and trefoil knots.

Observations

One example of Helaman Ferguson's work is *Umbilic Torus NC*. The work, which stands 27 inches high, was created by the manipulation of matrices associated with homogeneous cubic polynomials in two variables. With only one edge, you can trace the edge of *Umbilic Torus NC* three times around before returning to the starting point.

Purpose

In this lab, you will analyze Helaman Ferguson's work *Umbilic Torus NC*. You will use the *Derive* to aid you in your analysis.

References

For more information about mathematical sculptures see *Helaman Ferguson, Mathematics in Stone and Bronze* from Meridian Creative Group.

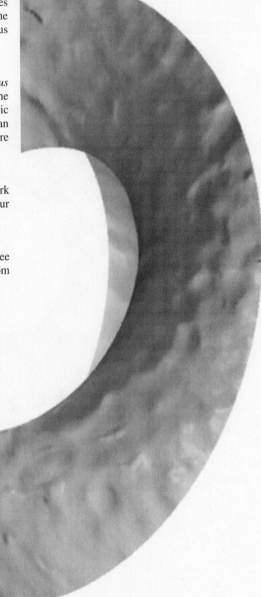

Helaman Ferguson's work *Umbilic Torus NC* is shown below. This form can be written as a parametric surface using the following set of parametric equations.

$$x = \sin u \left[7 + \cos\left(\frac{u}{3} - 2v\right) + 2 \cos\left(\frac{u}{3} + v\right) \right]$$

$$y = \cos u \left[7 + \cos\left(\frac{u}{3} - 2v\right) + 2 \cos\left(\frac{u}{3} + v\right) \right]$$

$$z = \sin\left(\frac{u}{3} - 2v\right) + 2 \sin\left(\frac{u}{3} + v\right)$$

$$-\pi \le u \le \pi, -\pi \le v \le \pi$$

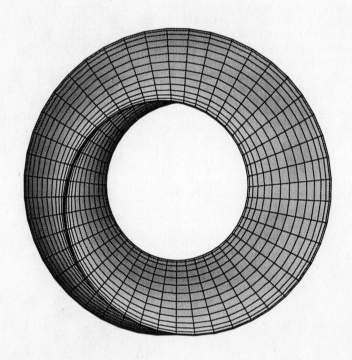

A graph of the parametric equations is stored in the *Derive* file called LAB1401.MTH. The instructions for this *Derive* file are stored in the text file called LAB1401.TXT.

Name _____

Date _____ Class _____

Instructor _____

1. *An "Elliptical" Torus.* When viewed along the z-axis, the torus appears nearly circular. Is it possible to alter this appearance so that the shape of the torus is more like that of an elongated ellipse? If so, explain how this could be done.

_____
_____
_____
_____
_____
_____
_____
_____
_____

2. *Comparing Graphs.* Explain how the umbilic torus shown in this lab's Data is similar to the Möbius strip shown below.

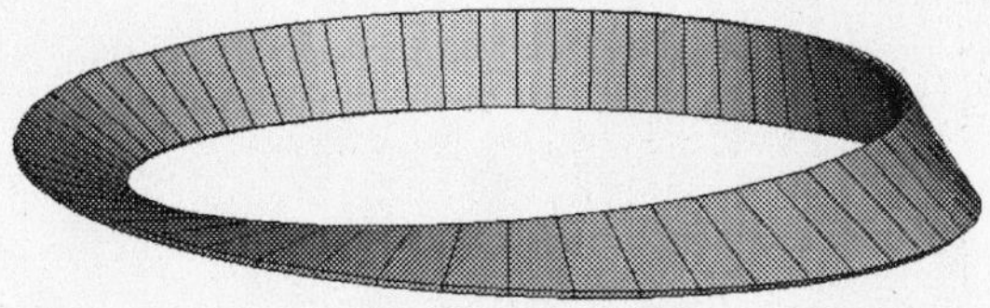

_____
_____
_____
_____
_____
_____
_____
_____

3. *Viewing the Torus From Different Points in Space.*   In this lab's Data, the point in space from which the umbilic torus is viewed is (0, 0, 10). Determine the point in space from which each graph of the umbilic torus below is viewed. Explain your strategy in determining the point of view.

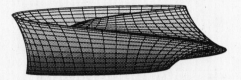

_____

_____

_____

_____

_____

_____

_____

4. *Cross Section.* An example of a cross-section of *Umbilic Torus NC* is shown below.

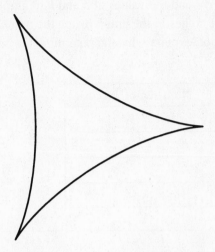

The cross-section is a hypocycloid with three arches. A hypocycloid is a curve generated by a point on the circumference of a circle rolling within the circumference of a larger circle. The parametric equations of a hypocycloid in the xy-plane are

$$x = (a - b) \cos \theta + b \cos \left[\frac{(a - b)\theta}{b} \right]$$

$$y = (a - b) \sin \theta - b \sin \left[\frac{(a - b)\theta}{b} \right]$$

where $0 \le \theta \le 2\pi$. One possible set of parametric equations of the hypocycloid shown above is as follows.

$$x = 2 \cos \theta + \cos 2\theta$$

$$y = 2 \cos \theta + \cos 2\theta$$

Use *Derive* to graph a hypocycloid with four arches and a hypocycloid with five arches. What values of a and b did you use to create your graphs? Determine the relationship between a and b for each of the following hypocycloids: one with three arches, one with four arches, and one with five arches. Determine the relationship between a and b for a hypocycloid with n arches.

_____

_____

_____

_____

_____

5. *Complete the Table.* Use the relationship from Exercise 4 and the values of *a* and *b* in the table to predict the number of arches each hypocycloid has. Then use *Derive* and the values of *a* and *b* to graph each hypocycloid. Does the number of arches in the graph match the number of arches predicted in the table? If not, explain why and determine the correct relationship between *a* and *b*.

a	b	Number of Arches
8	2	
21	7	
18	3	
20	4	

_____

_____

_____

_____

_____

_____

6. *Graphing the Torus Using Different Ranges.* The graph of the umbilic torus below was created using the same set of parametric equations given in this lab's Data, except that one of the parameter ranges used was altered, as was the point in space from which the umbilic torus was viewed. Determine which parameter range was changed and what the parameter's new range is. Then determine the new point in space from which the umbilic torus is viewed.

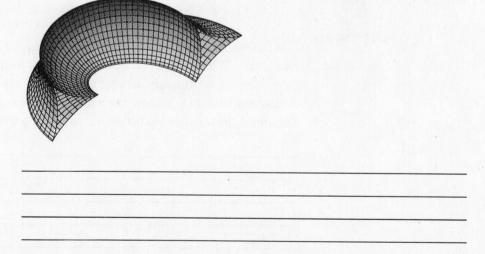

_____

_____

_____

_____

_____

LAB 15.1

INTERACTING POPULATIONS
Euler's Method

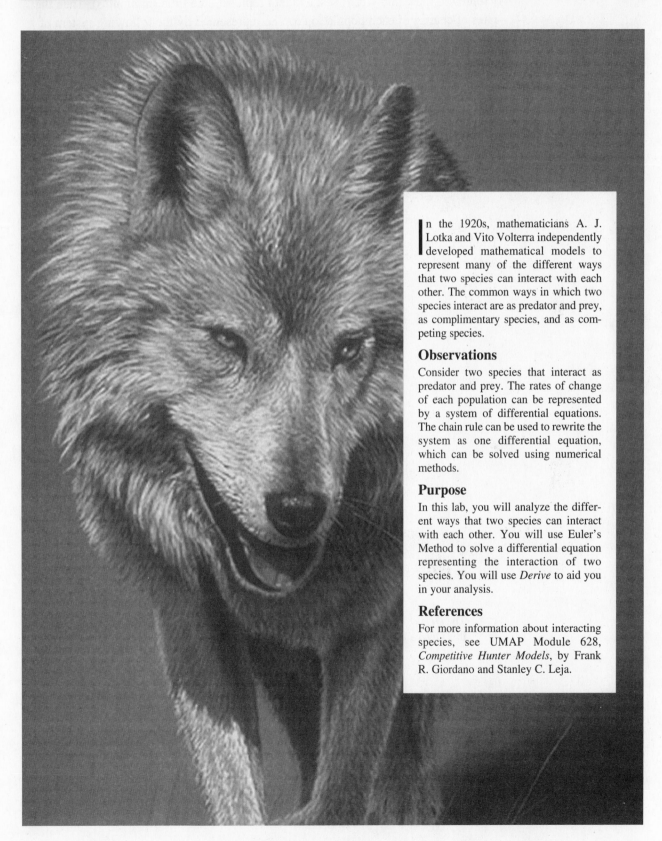

In the 1920s, mathematicians A. J. Lotka and Vito Volterra independently developed mathematical models to represent many of the different ways that two species can interact with each other. The common ways in which two species interact are as predator and prey, as complimentary species, and as competing species.

Observations

Consider two species that interact as predator and prey. The rates of change of each population can be represented by a system of differential equations. The chain rule can be used to rewrite the system as one differential equation, which can be solved using numerical methods.

Purpose

In this lab, you will analyze the different ways that two species can interact with each other. You will use Euler's Method to solve a differential equation representing the interaction of two species. You will use *Derive* to aid you in your analysis.

References

For more information about interacting species, see UMAP Module 628, *Competitive Hunter Models*, by Frank R. Giordano and Stanley C. Leja.

Consider a predator and prey relationship involving foxes and rabbits. The rabbits are a food source for the foxes, so the rabbits are the prey and the foxes are the predator in this relationship. Let x represent the number of rabbits, let y represent the number of foxes, and let t represent the time (in months). Then the rates of change of each population can be represented by the following system of differential equations. (In this system, a, b, m, and n are positive constants.)

$$\frac{dx}{dt} = ax - bxy \text{ and } \frac{dy}{dt} = -my + nxy$$

These equations have many possible solutions that can be obtained by solving the following differential equation.

$$\frac{dy}{dx} = \frac{dy/dt}{dx/dt} = \frac{-my + nxy}{ax - bxy}$$

The particular solutions depend on the initial values of x and y and on the values of a, b, m, and n.

The *Derive* file corresponding to this lab is called LAB1501.MTH. The instructions for this *Derive* file are stored in the text file called LAB1501.TXT.

Name _____

Date _____ Class _____

Instructor _____

1. **Euler's Method.** Consider the differential equation $y' = F(x, y)$ with the initial condition $y(x_0) = y_0$. At any point in the domain of F, $F(x_k, y_k)$ yields the slope of the solution at that point. Euler's Method gives a discrete set of estimates of the y-values of a solution of the differential equation using the iterative formula

$$y_{k+1} = y_k + F(x_k, y_k)\Delta x$$

where $\Delta x = x_{k+1} - x_k$. Given that a certain predator and prey relationship can be modeled by

$$y' = \frac{-0.3y + 0.006xy}{0.8x - 0.04xy}$$

with $(x_0, y_0) = (55, 10)$ where the prey population x and predator population y are measured in hundreds, use Euler's Method to approximate the value of y and complete the table below. Describe the change in the predator population y as the prey population x grows. Which population appears to be changing at a faster rate?

k	x	y
0	55	10
1	80	
2	105	

_____

_____

_____

_____

_____

_____

_____

_____

2. *The Magnitude of* Δx. In Exercise 1, the y-values were estimated using $\Delta x = 25$. Describe how decreasing the magnitude of Δx affects the accuracy of Euler's Method.

_____

_____

_____

_____

_____

_____

_____

3. *Using Derive to do Euler's Method.* Use *Derive* to approximate the value of y for the predator-prey model given in Exercise 1 for $55 \leq x \leq 105$ and $\Delta x = 5$. Compare the results of each table and explain any differences. Did decreasing the magnitude of Δx affect the accuracy of Euler's Method? If so, what was the effect?

_____

_____

_____

_____

_____

_____

_____

_____

4. *Graphing the Results.* Use *Derive* to graph the results of Exercises 1 and 3 together. Which graph do you think better models the interacting populations? *Derive* can be used to solve differential equations. Use *Derive* to graph a solution of the model given in Exercise 1 and compare it to the graphs of the other results.

_____

_____

_____

_____

_____

_____

_____

5. *Reasonable Assumptions?* Some of the assumptions made about the predator and prey populations described in this lab's Data are listed below. Discuss the reasonableness of each assumption.

- The prey has an abundant food supply.

  _____

  _____

  _____

  _____

  _____

  _____

  _____

- The predator feeds exclusively on the prey.

  _____

  _____

  _____

  _____

  _____

  _____

  _____

- The environment can support unlimited quantities of the prey.

  _____

  _____

  _____

  _____

  _____

  _____

  _____

- There is no need to consider females and males separately.

  _____

  _____

  _____

  _____

  _____

  _____

  _____

6. *Considering the Limits.*   What if the environment can't support unlimited quantities of the prey? Does this limit the size of the predator population? Explain.

_____

_____

_____

_____

_____

_____

_____

7. *Do They Die Out?*   Consider the set of differential equations

$$\frac{dx}{dt} = ax - bxy \ \text{ and } \ \frac{dy}{dt} = -my + nxy$$

modeling a prey population and a predator population, respectively. Is there a point where the prey or predator populations die out? If so, list a point where this situation occurs. What do you think happens to the prey population if the predator population is eliminated? Is there a point where both populations die out?

_____

_____

_____

_____

_____

_____

_____

8. *Using Different Initial Values.*   Use *Derive* to repeat Exercise 1 for different initial values. Explain what happens to the quantities of both populations when the initial values are the same.

_____

_____

_____

_____

_____

_____

_____